What Husbands & Wives Aren't Telling Each Other

Steve & Annie
CHAPMAN

HARVEST HOUSE™ PUBLISHERS
EUGENE, OREGON

Cover by Koechel Peterson & Associates, Inc., Minneapolis, Minnesota

WHAT HUSBANDS AND WIVES AREN'T TELLING EACH OTHER

Copyright © 2003 by Steve and Annie Chapman
Published by Harvest House Publishers
Eugene, Oregon 97402
www.harvesthousepublishers.com

Library of Congress Cataloging-in-Publication Data
Chapman, Steve.
    What husbands and wives aren't telling each other / Steve and Annie Chapman.
       p. cm.
    ISBN 0-7369-1182-0 (pbk.)
    1. Communication in marriage. 2. Marital conflict. 3. Man–woman relationships. I. Chapman, Annie.
    II. Title.
HQ734.C48 2003
306.872—dc21   2003002451

Printed in the United States of America.

03 04 05 06 07 08 09 10 11 / BP-CF / 10 9 8 7 6 5 4 3 2 1

This book is dedicated especially to
our children and their spouses,
Emmitt and Heidi Beall,
married 11-25-00,
and
Nathan and Stephanie Chapman,
married 10-27-01.

Acknowledgments

A special thanks to all the husbands and wives who were kind enough to respond to our questionnaire. Without your vulnerability in sharing your deepest feelings, this book could not have been written.

Contents

The Meat-Loaf Revelation

Annie: For the first two years of our marriage I made meat loaf. What all-American family doesn't eat this traditional dish at least once a week? One day, while I was preparing my grocery list, I asked Steve, "Would you like to have meat loaf tonight?" He replied, "No, I don't like meat loaf."

My response was one of shock. I said, "For the past two years you have eaten meat loaf every week. Why didn't you tell me you don't like it?" He answered, "You didn't ask me."

How many couples are going through life with belly aches because the simplest of thoughts are not shared? As a result of silence, they are not enjoying their marriage to the full extent. Still, they never ask or volunteer how they feel or what desires they might possess. There comes a point in the relationship between a husband and wife when it's time to stop being miserable, cease complaining, and start telling the other person what you want. After Steve told me he didn't like meat loaf, I never made it again (when he was home, anyway). Was I trying to complicate his life by feeding him something he didn't want? Of course not. Nor was he trying to play the role of the meat-loaf martyr. We simply didn't communicate about the subject.

Going back through the years I wondered if there were other unaddressed "issues" in our marriage. What else had Steve silently swallowed even though he didn't like it? As I pondered the question, I realized that in our nearly three decades together there were indeed other meat-loaf revelations that were discovered. And with each one, our relationship grew stronger and sweeter.

For example, it took some time before I could tell my outdoor-loving husband that I really didn't enjoy riding a bicycle along a busy highway. I was not a big fan of the outside mirrors of passing cars and trucks that would barely miss my handlebars as they sped by. My nerves just couldn't take it. Nor did I care for that pin-sized seat on the bike he bought for me…us…to enjoy. Try as I did to like it, my constant squeezing of the brake levers and the accompanying little frantic screams during the downhills didn't contribute much to our having fun. Finally, I had to say something about it. I had to let him know that my idea of a thrill did not include a 40 MPH "fall" off a steep, paved, Tennessee incline as my eye sockets filled up with water!

Thankfully, he took it well. Once Steve understood my reservations about using danger as recreational therapy, he treated my appreciation of the outdoors quite differently. To this day, I am convinced that my willingness to help him see my fears assisted him in altering his expectations in regard to my participation in outside adventures. My willingness to open up about my dread of bicycle "road rash" resulted in the best gardening buddy I have today.

Steve was able to see that my preference for enjoying God's creation is my flower garden. Instead of having a husband who grumbles about me rarely leaving my backyard for adventure, I have a man who, each year on Mother's Day, gives me a most wonderful gift—mulch. That's right! Steve mulches my garden. But the best part is that he mulches and never complains.

Having seen the immeasurable value of a husband and wife experiencing their own meat-loaf revelations like we did, and seeing the rewards of the communication that can follow, we have been motivated to write this book. Rest assured, this text is about much more than dinner items, bicycles, and mulch. These pages address many other subjects that are of great concern but, perhaps, to date, they have not been discussed by spouses.

In order to find out what spouses wanted or needed to be saying to each other, for the past year we have asked approximately 500 couples from all parts of the country to complete a questionnaire we developed for this book. The pages ahead of you contain many of their responses marked by a ✶ .

The input from those who put their hearts on paper was fascinating. First of all, we discovered that marrieds remain silent for reasons that range from being afraid to talk to being convinced that if they did, it wouldn't do any good. However, when it came to what husbands and wives were keeping to themselves, we discovered that many people were not saying the same things.

We want to give you a glimpse of what others are saying, including our own insights from our marriage. In so doing, you might see yourself in the thoughts of others and find the courage to form your own words about the issues. In addition to revealing some of the things not being said, we offer some helpful direction regarding the subjects. May God bless you as you discover and discuss what husbands and wives aren't telling each other.

one

Prepared, Repaired, Paired

Did you ever hear the story about the near-sighted snake who got married? Later he bought himself a pair of glasses. When he put them on, and looked at his wife, he realized he'd married a garden hose!

There are far too many husbands and wives who have experienced that kind of shock when it comes to their mates. Thinking they had married their perfect match, they later discovered that's exactly what they got—a lifeless stick of wood with no fire.

The truth is, none of us really knows the one we marry. Not completely. Steve and I met in junior high in 1963, went through high school together, and lived only eight miles apart. We even shared some of the same friends. Yet there was no way at the ripe young age of our early twenties that we could have made a fully rational decision to confidently commit to a lifelong union. Love had certainly blurred our vision.

In truth, marriage is one of the biggest risks anyone ever takes, no matter how well acquainted the two people might be. We nearly shiver today to think of how little we actually knew about the other. Still, we exchanged vows and promised to walk through the remainder of our time side by side.

How did it turn out? We will answer by confessing something we know might be difficult for some folks to accept. We do so with a certain amount of anticipation that our credibility might be damaged in

11

some doubtful hearts. But here goes: We confess that our married years have been the absolute best of our lives. We are—brace yourself—happily married! As one husband said, "I'm so happy being married to this woman it would make a freight train take a dirt road!" We're not sure exactly what he meant by his quip, but the gleam in his eyes told us he was a happy man.

You may be wondering, "How can it be that you have found such happiness?" First, each of us arrived at our wedding day on March 29, 1975, as two people who had given their lives to Jesus Christ. Gratefully, both of us knew in the deep recesses of our hearts that our greatest need was not the humanness in the other person. Instead, we each brought to the altar an awareness that our all-encompassing necessity as individuals was our spiritual need for a Savior.

As a young bride and groom, we stood before the preacher that sunny spring day with only the best intentions of fulfilling the other's dreams. However, it was to our advantage to know that complete contentment in this life is dependent upon God's presence in us. We knew that we needed to allow God to daily create in us a clean heart so that we could live at peace with Him (see Psalm 51:10). Without hesitation we can say that it was the individual pursuit of a relationship with Christ that contributed most to the oneness we experienced as newlyweds. It remains true today.

Herein lies the most important thing that far too many husbands and wives are not telling each other:

> "I want to meet your deepest needs and be your dreammate, but as a weak human being I cannot do it. I know very well that is a God-sized job. I am quite aware, however, that even though I don't have the power to make you happy, I can make your life miserable and even be a hindrance to God's work of peace in your heart. As much as I would like to help you, only He can make your spirit smile forever."

If this is indeed the top statement that spouses have left unspoken, why is it so often unsaid? In many cases, the answer involves an innocent unawareness. Even though the men or women might have made sincere and noble promises to make their mates happy, they simply did not know that it is God alone who can and wants to be the ultimate source of bliss.

Though we were fortunate that it was early on in our relationship that we embraced our human limitations, it was not until more than 20 years of marriage had passed that we were able to verbalize it. Using the valuable tool of retrospect, the following describes our journey to the marriage altar.

Prepared

First, God *prepared* us for each other. After He created man and assessed the situation, He proclaimed that something was amiss. He looked at Adam and addressed his need by saying, "It is not good for the man to be alone" (Genesis 2:18). Adam's problem was not one of sin because at the time God said, "It is not good," His first man was in a sinless condition. Nor was Adam's dilemma an environmental problem since he was living in the Garden of Eden, a perfect physical world. Instead, God saw that man was suffering from solitude. So, the Creator prepared some company for Adam. Her name was Eve. Thus it was from the beginning that husbands and wives are made for each other. Drawing on our music background, the following lyric expresses our gratitude for God's incredible plan.

We

If He hadn't made you
If He hadn't made me
There wouldn't be us
And we couldn't say we.
There had to be one
So there could be two
So He could make one
Out of me and you.

Two ships
One shore
Two dancers
One floor
Two birds flying in one sky of blue
Baby, that's me and you.

Where do you end
And where do I start
It's hard to tell when God puts two hearts
Together
It doesn't get any better.[1]

Repaired

God not only *prepared* us but He also *repaired* us.

Husbands and wives are like the two halves of a modular home we saw arriving by truck to a setup site in our county. The huge, preformed structures were very nice in their appearance but the strong wind created by their journey down the Tennessee highways had ripped roofing off of one half and some siding off the other. Before the workmen joined the two parts, there was some rebuilding that needed to be done.

It is safe to say that, like the two halves of that modular home, nearly all of us have experienced some kind of emotional damage in the years prior to our wedding days.

To illustrate, the following statements are taken from a few of the questionnaires that were completed. The inquiry was, "What emotions do you struggle with the most as a married person, and where do you think they originated?"

- Worthlessness. My mom would only accept a boy when she was pregnant with me. I was a disappointment to her. To make matters worse, I was born with a defective kidney that had to be removed. The medical attention and the expense of it all caused a great deal of ongoing stress in her. I have never measured up in my mom's eyes. (Wife—married 18 years)

- Guilt. As a little girl I was tortured by an older brother. I fight hatred for him to this day. (Wife—married 36 years)

- Inferiority. My father never gave me recognition of my worth to him. I tried desperately to make him proud, but I don't think it ever happened. (Wife—33 years)

- I feel depressed most of the time, and I'm sure being unable to ever please my mother has a lot to do with it. (Wife—11 years)

- I came from a home where incest happened until I was 18 years old and left home. I was beaten, and I struggle now to forgive my dad. (Wife—25 years)

- I don't remember ever being hugged or told I was loved as a child. I grew up with a martyr complex. (Wife—12 years)

- My dad was an alcoholic and his beatings of me and my siblings is too hard to forget. (Husband—22 years)

- If I ever did anything to bring a smile to my dad's face, I don't remember it. I have dealt with sadness about this for a lot of years. (Husband—married 18 years)

- An older neighbor sexually took advantage of me when I was around six years old. Shame and hatred are the emotions I have fought since my childhood. (Husband—married 28 years)

- The memories of watching my dad beat my mother still haunts me. (Husband—14 years)

- Being teased as a kid because of my weight makes it tough to allow anyone to get close to me. (Husband—married 16 years)

- My dad beat me badly one day and then locked me in a closet for hours. I have never pardoned him for it, but I'm not sure if I can. (Husband—married 28 years)

These responses are, to say the least, heart wrenching. Several of these individuals indicated on their questionnaires that they were also divorced and remarried. That information about their history seemed to be a commentary on the likelihood that their unresolved childhood struggles had a negative effect on their relationships in later years.

While not all of those who answered the question noted such excruciating memories of their past, the high numbers that did (7 out of 10) reveals a disturbing pattern. Most of us were in need of repairs prior to saying those two unforgettable words, "I do." We would like to report that we fall into the 3 out of 10 category of those who were fortunate to have reached marrying age damage free. However, it would not be the truth.

Annie: I was raised on a family-owned-and-operated farm that required the occasional hiring of itinerant workers. When I was five years old, one of the buildings I enjoyed playing in as a child was used by one of the hired hands as a trap where he cruelly raped me.

. Though the man was arrested, the trial judge handed down a very light punishment as he said, "Why should we disrupt this man's life with something this child will soon forget." Unfortunately, his thinking was typical of the times.

The problem was, I never forgot the incident. In fact, the result was that I eventually began a journey down the dangerous road of rage. [For more of my story, read *A Woman's Answer to Anger* (Harvest House, 2002).]

Steve: When I was around seven years old, my mother took me along with her to visit another mom in the neighborhood. There was no way she could have known what awaited me in that home. While playing out of her sight with the neighbor's son, who was a little older, I was shown a Polaroid pornographic picture that was rather explicit for the 1950s.

That day, I was a little boy who had been introduced to a man-sized battle. Sadly, the years that followed were filled with mental moral struggles that sent me into a spiritual tailspin.

How utterly grateful we both are that God, in His rich love toward us, had mercy on our union by doing some careful repair work on these and other areas of our hearts and minds prior to our marriage. What a wonderful thought that He, as the Master Repairman, was able to mend the damage that life had caused to our "modular halves." We are convinced that having allowed Him to mend the brokenness in our hearts before our marriage on March 29, 1975, is the key to our longevity as a couple.

We must add that in no way does this testimony imply that God never again had to do another repair job in our lives. The fact is, as we continue to allow Him to assess the condition of our hearts, the occasional repairs still have to be done. The weathering effects of life's challenges such as fighting and losing battles against sinful temptations, trying to make financial ends meet, parenting, offenses against us, and fears of an uncertain future are a few of the winds that rip at our roofing and tear at our siding. Allowing the Master Repairman to do His work is paramount to our survival, even though it requires a certain level of vulnerability before Him. The psalmist David provided the words to one of the most important prayers that we, as a husband and wife, can offer: "Search me, O God, and know my heart; try me and know my anxious thoughts; and see if there be any hurtful way in me, and lead me in the everlasting way" (Psalm 139:23-24). In addition, we take comfort in the promise found in Philippians 1:6 NKJV: "Being confident of this very thing, that He who has begun a good work in you will complete it until the day of Jesus Christ."

There may be a spouse who, at this moment, is reading our story and is asking, "I am already married and the damage, even since childhood, has never been repaired. Is it too late for me?" With great joy and excitement we say, "Absolutely not!" At any moment in the framework of time, people can present their broken, betrayed, or emotionally bleeding hearts to Christ, and He can mend and restore them. At this hour, Jesus is saying to you through the writings of Luke: "The Spirit of the LORD is upon Me, because He has anointed Me to preach the gospel to the poor; He has sent Me to heal the brokenhearted, to proclaim liberty to the captives and recovery of sight to the blind, to set at liberty those who are oppressed; to proclaim the acceptable year of the LORD" (Luke 4:18-19 NKJV).

May we suggest that wherever you are on the trail of time, if you haven't already done so, that you present yourself to God and allow Him the opportunity to "fix your half of the modular"? Whatever damage might have been done, or is being done, give the job to Christ. If you decide to do so, we must offer a warning along with a word of encouragement.

Knowing from experience that God's initial work of restoration in your heart has two distinct parts to it, we must tell you that the process is not an easy one. Yet, if you allow Him to do this twofold work in your spirit, it could do the absolute most in setting into motion a restoration of the joy you long for as an individual and in your marriage. It is found in being forgiven and forgiving.

To confess that we are in need of our Savior and to receive His pardon for sin is the initial work God wants to do in every heart (Romans 4:7-8). *After* we are blessed with so great a pardon, He wants to help us return that grace to others. Matthew 6:12 NKJV reveals that process: "forgive us our debts, as we forgive our debtors." Another passage that makes this progression clear is Colossians 3:12-13 NKJV: "Therefore, as the elect of God, holy and beloved, put on tender mercies, kindness, humility, meekness, longsuffering; bearing with one another, and forgiving one another, if anyone has a complaint against another; *even as Christ forgave you, so you also must do*" (emphasis added).

For the one who was hurt to experience complete healing, forgiveness of that transgressor must follow being forgiven, no matter how unworthy the offender may be. In our case, showing the mercy of Christ to a rapist and a neighbor who was a peddler of porn was paramount to the healing that took place in our hearts before we reached our wedding day.

We are confident that had we not forgiven the ones who had been used as instruments of Satan to wreak havoc on our halves of the home, we would have entered into our marriage with our emotional hands bound behind our backs, unable to fully embrace the other. It would have not been a great way to begin.

Perhaps unforgiveness is the bondage you feel in your heart at this time. So many of the individuals who exposed the depths of their hearts on our questionnaires expressed an ongoing war with emotions such as bitterness. Undeniably, their relationship with their mates suffered because of it, even for some into 40 and 50 years of their marriage. How sad.

Accepting the forgiveness of Christ and extending that grace to others was the key to setting us free to love and be loved. But turning that key required an act of our will. May you find courage to do the same. We urge you to read, memorize, and act upon the tender truth found in Romans 5:8: "But God demonstrates His own love toward us, in that while we were yet sinners, Christ died for us." May the unconditional love He bestows to you be the motivation you need to use the key of forgiveness. (For more information and guidance on the steps to forgiveness, see Annie's book *A Woman's Answer to Anger*.)

Paired

Moving on, God first *prepared* us, then *repaired* us, and it was *then* that He *paired* us. When we look back through our years, we can see that it was this divine progression that has contributed most to the quality of our home. We hope you, too, will experience the sweet reward we have enjoyed from being willing to allow God the freedom to be with us throughout the years.

The Foundation

Drawing once more from the "marriage is a modular home" analogy, one other part of the setup process of this type of home would be valuable to look at. When two modular halves are delivered to the site, there is something already in place. It was there well before the "wedding" of the two parts. That preexisting structure was the block foundation.

How senseless it would have been to go to the effort to deliver two expensive halves of the home to this site in our neighborhood and then place them on unstable dirt. Wisely, the block foundation had been built and was ready, willing, and "longing" for the "couple" to rest on it.

What a beautiful picture of our Father in heaven who has been there forever, willing for the two of us to place all the weight of our lives on Him. As a married couple we cherish the passage in 1 Corinthians 3:11 that comforts us with these words: "...For no man can lay a foundation other than the one which is laid, which is Jesus Christ." He alone is our foundation, the stone that our house sits upon. The rewards of fulfilling our responsibility in terms of doing things God's way are revealed in Matthew 7:24-25: "Therefore whoever hears these sayings of Mine, and does them, I will liken him to a wise man who built his house on the rock; and the rain descended, the floods came, and the winds blew and beat on that house; and it did not fall, for it was founded on the rock." Knowing that God holds our house safely on the solid foundation of His love is the reason we can face the storms of this life.

How about your lives as individuals and as a couple? On what do you rest yourself and your home? Is it the raw, sinking, unsteady ground of this world? Or have you placed your lives on Christ, the solid rock?

The following lyric is about our house. These words are not about a house made of wood, nails, brick, and mortar. Instead, they describe two hearts that have survived the threatening weather that this world can throw at us. It was written to celebrate our silver anniversary that took place in the year of 2000. The words are still true for us.

This House Still Stands

It started as a rumble
Turned into a roar
Do you remember how that wind
Pounded on our door?
We lost some shingles
We lost a window pane
But when that storm had passed us
This old house remained.

This house still stands
This house still stands
We built it on the Rock
We didn't build it on the sand
This house still stands

It started as a teardrop
And turned into a flood
When troubles came to wash away
These walls that hold our love
But, babe, do you remember
How we called on Jesus' name
And when that flood had passed us
This old house remained.

This house still stands
This house still stands
We built it on the Rock
We didn't build it on the sand
This house still stands.[2]

two

I Need a Teammate, Not a Cell Mate

J.J. Jasper, a friend in Mississippi, called one day and with a tone of distress in his voice, said, "Steve and Annie, please pray for my uncle up in Kentucky. He manages the circus and a couple of years ago he married the woman who does the human cannonball stunt. Well, she up and left him for the lion tamer. He was all tore up when he called and said, 'I'll never find another woman of her caliber!'" (All the hunters will get this one right away.)

Now, there's a picture of a fellow who had come to an important resolve. He was willing to admit that in order for the "show to go on" he needed his wife. As stated in the previous chapter, it is a smart thing for any "Adam" to agree with God that he is made better by the company of his "Eve." However, the reverse can also be true. A woman's life can be enriched and more productive when she is joined to her man.

For the purposes of planting this seed of truth in the hearts of couples who come to our concerts, we perform a love song entitled, "I Need You." In nearly every setting, we ask the husbands and wives to sing the words of the title to one another. As they do, the view of the audience from our perspective is quite interesting. Most women are quick to respond and with little trouble they look toward their husbands and sing. Many of those men, however, will look straight ahead and tentatively mouth the words. If they turn their faces at all toward their

21

wives, they do so in such a way that it makes it look as though their necks are in braces. We can't help but feel a bit of sorrow for the wives.

To be fair, we also observe women who struggle to publicly proclaim "I need you" to their husbands. We see excited expressions on the men's faces. It's a look that seems to come from the anticipation that he will hear her serenade him with her angelic voice of desire for his company. Sadly, their smiles are too often turned upside down by her obvious lack of enthusiasm.

While we suspect, of course, that their hesitance to sing is a product of shyness or stage fright (or, in some cases, "pew fright"), there are a significant number of spouses whose openly hostile body language reveals a more serious cause for their choice to not join the choir. Folded arms, jaws that are set, and lips that flatly refuse to move are disconcerting sights to look at while we sing. We fear that their lack of participation represents something that some of these husbands and wives are *not* saying to each other:

> "I know that in order for our marriage to be a success, we need to work at it together. But it's hard to feel like your teammate when there are times you make me feel more like a cell mate. To sing 'I need you' is not so easy when I feel hopelessly locked behind the bars of matrimony."

The silent singers, it seems, have resigned themselves to the idea that marriage is indeed an *institution*, and they feel like they have received a "life sentence"! Why are we concerned this may be true for far too many couples? The following statements show the reason we would make this disturbing assessment. We asked, "What does your spouse do that makes you feel miserable?"

Women

- When I ask a question, he often makes me feel dumb.

- When there's a problem he usually shuts down and won't discuss it.

- He sits and watches TV and never asks if I need help and never offers.

- Sometimes he cuts me with sarcasm, and then says, "I'm only kidding."

- He brings his pressure at work home with him.

- He sits at his computer and plays games and surfs the Internet when he should be helping me.

- When he jokes about my homemaking and says it's not a "real" job.

- When he hugs other women in a suggestive manner.

- He neglects his physical health.

- Very often he leaves a mess and expects me to clean up after him.

- When he talks about my weight to other people and calls me "fat."

Men

- She snaps at me and puts me under tremendous pressure.

- Belittles me in front of friends and family.

- Complains about nearly everything.

- Expects me to be romantic, and yet never gives me a gift or reciprocates in any way.

- She never seems to be satisfied with the work I do around the house.

- I get accused a lot of looking at other women. She is unjustifiably jealous and controlling.

- She treats me like an enemy instead of her friend.

- She commits adultery.

- I get the silent treatment a lot.

- She tells me I've hurt her and then doesn't tell me what I did.

- She tears down my vocation.

- She never cleans the house.

- She bosses me around and tells me every move to make. I feel like her boy instead of her man.

In light of these anonymous, but painfully true confessions, it is not too difficult to understand why some husbands and wives feel more like fellow inmates than intimates. How grievous it is to hear of their gaping emotional wounds caused by the shank of unkindness and lack of cooperation. It is no wonder that the words "I need you" would be the last song any of them would want to sing to the other.

In order for these husbands and wives to regain that special freedom to be colaborers, the shackles of mistreatment that one places on the other need to fall away from their hearts. If they are able to break the "bondages of marriage," they can then enjoy the "bonds of matrimony" and become a prize-winning team. For that reason we offer the following key that might help remove those fetters.

If You Know Better, You'll Do Better

We learned many years ago that motive dictates motion, attitude affects action, or, to put it another way, if you know better, you'll do better. (*Steve:* As an example, remember our meat-loaf revelation? By communicating with Annie, she knows me better—and I'm happy to say that I haven't had to eat meat loaf in years!)

Perhaps the single most attitude-altering instruction that we received as a newlywed couple came from the late Archie and Margaret Boone, the parents of well-known singer Pat Boone. In 1975, they told us, "Make your home look like a wagon wheel. Put Christ at the hub. Make Him the center of your lives. Then, as you follow the line of the spokes, notice that as they get closer to the hub, they grow closer to one another. This will work for you even if you're opposites in personality!"

The natural inclination for a young bride and groom is to try to grow closer by exclusively focusing on the other, desiring to solely please their mate. While this traditional approach to building a strong unit certainly has its merits, we have found a more lasting and rewarding method.

As two people walk side by side with a mutual focus on pleasing Christ, their hearts will begin to look like the spokes in a wheel that get closer to each other as they get closer to the hub. Making Christ the focal point in a marriage is the key. So simple is this concept, but so incredibly profound.

How does maintaining a desire to please Christ become the motivation that can influence our actions toward each other? The answer to that question is found in Philippians 2. In verse five of the chapter, God's people are encouraged to "have this attitude in yourselves which was also in Christ Jesus." To learn what that attitude was, it is necessary to read the four previous verses. As you read this passage, please do so in light of our premise that suggests to spouses, "If you know better, you'll do better!"

> Therefore if there is any encouragement in Christ, if there is any consolation of love, if there is any fellowship of the Spirit, if any affection and compassion, make my joy complete by being of the same mind, maintaining the same love, united in spirit, intent on one purpose. Do nothing from selfishness or empty conceit, but with humility of mind let each of you regard one another as more important than yourselves; do not merely look out for your own personal interests, but also for the interests of others (Philippians 2:1-4).

Putting the happiness of others before that of His own was the attitude of Christ. His selfless demonstration of love generates much of the honor we give to Him today. However, that praise was gained at a great price. It is revealed in verses 6-8.

> Who, although He existed in the form of God did not regard equality with God a thing to be grasped, but emptied Himself, taking the form of a bond-servant, and being made in the likeness of men. Being found in appearance as a man, He humbled Himself by becoming obedient to the point of death, even death on a cross.

How do we practically apply this passage to our everyday married lives? We are, by no means, suggesting that spouses crucify each other, though some who have been sufficiently hurt may have considered it. Instead, as we stated in the previous chapter, each member of the team must be responsible to individually strive to become like Christ, whose servant attitude caused Him to focus on the needs of others. In our own lives, we have seen what this spiritual truth can look like when clothed in flesh.

Dishes and Turkeys

Our personal interests are quite varied.

Annie: "I love beautiful china dishes."

Steve: "I love little animals. I think they're delicious. I love to hunt them down, kill them, and eat them."

Obviously the pendulum of passions swings wide in our relationship. Yet personally striving to maintain the servant attitude of Christ makes all the difference in the face of our vast differences. The following true accounts demonstrate how God's truth in Philippians 2 can be transferred from principles on paper to practical performance.

Annie: Steve was very saddened when he realized one year that the date of our March wedding anniversary inconveniently fell on the first day of Tennessee's turkey hunting season. His buddies were also upset that "Stevie wasn't gonna get to come out and play!" In the past, they had looked forward to gathering at a cabin the night before opening day of season and enjoying an evening of food and preparation for the next morning's hunt.

As I pondered what gift I would get him for our anniversary it suddenly occurred to me that I had an opportunity to win at the "game" we had made of Philippians 2, that is, trying to out-serve one another. (This game, by the way, is fun only if both play to win!) I decided that my gift would be to encourage him to join his friends for the hunt and delay our celebration until the next evening. I sent him to the cabin with food, the admonition to have a great time, and my regular safety speech that would ensure his return.

The morning of our anniversary came, and I headed to town to run some errands. I came home around noon and made a surprising discovery. Steve had left the hunt early, came home, and was standing high on a ladder cleaning our second-story windows. (He claims that he stood on that ladder for nearly an hour, waiting for me to see him in his servant pose when I pulled into the driveway. He was determined not to lose "the game.")

Steve: Annie came home from town one day and told me about a set of china dishes she adored. The pattern contained red birds and reminded her of her mother's love for the cardinal. Since her mother's death, she has enjoyed collecting items that feature that particular feathered friend. I told Annie to go and buy them, but she adamantly declined to do so due to their hefty price tag.

Then one day, while traveling through Ohio, we had a few extra minutes and we stopped at an outlet center (the real kind of outlet that has stores that actually have discounts). We went into a china shop and lo and behold, there were the dishes marked with significant discounts. I begged Annie to get them, but again she hesitated. So I began to rummage through the shopping carts that were filled with the dishes, finding the very best pieces. With a ten-place setting now stacked on the checkout counter, I turned to her and said words that made her eyes dance with excitement. "You have to have the teapot!"

I left the store that day a hero. Annie told me later that if men knew how sexually stimulating it is for a woman to see her man going through stacks of dishes to buy for her, there would be warehouses of china behind every home. She said she couldn't wait to get me back to the house!

One of the most treasured realizations that resulted from these two accounts can be explained in this way: *It looked like dishes…but it felt like love. It looked like a turkey hunt…but it felt like love.* When a husband and wife take to heart the challenge of serving one another and consider the interest of the other as more important than their own, the end result is that each feels loved. Again, this is the attitude of Christ in that He gave His very life for us. In other words, *it looked like a cross, but it felt like love!*

Besides dishes and turkey hunts, there are many other things that two people can do for each other that will display the servant heart of Christ. These married couples responded to the question: "What does your mate do or say that makes you feel happy?"

Wives

- My husband asks my opinion in front of others.
- He compliments me on the way I look. He tells me I'm pretty.
- I love it when my husband says, "I'm glad I married you."
- He helps me with the housework without being asked.
- I appreciate when he recognizes special occasions without me reminding him.
- He loves and adopted my children. When he treats my children kindly, I feel loved.
- His support for me when I try something new helps me have the confidence to try other things.

- Sometimes when I'm troubled he'll say, "Do you want me to pray for you?" And then he does.

- He hugs me for no reason, just to let me know he loves me.

- He tells me that he loves me and compliments me on the job I do as a mother.

- I love it when he comes quickly to the door and greets me by saying, "There's my sweetheart. How was your day?"

Husbands

- She thanks me for doing special things to help her. It makes me want to do more.

- I love it when she makes me coffee.

- Goes out with me…without the children.

- Plans a special time for just the two of us.

- She understands my stress load at work. She makes sure I have some relaxing time in the evening. I feel cared for when she looks out for me like that.

- My wife picks out my clothes and buys them for me so I don't have to go shopping.

- Shows an interest in sex.

- My wife doesn't give me a hard time about my obligations at work. I can't help the workload that's put on me, and I need her supportive attitude. I couldn't survive without her help.

- She listens to me vent about work without always feeling like she has to give me advice or her opinions.

- She thanks me for providing for her and the children.

- When my laundry is clean and put away, I feel so loved and taken care of.

- Every night she greets me with a hug and a kiss. I feel like she's glad I'm home.

* My wife gives unsolicited physical contact in the form of shoulder and foot massages. How good can it get!

* My wife tells me she's so glad I'm in her life. Her words mean a lot to me.

As we read the words of these husbands and wives, we can almost hear their songs of joy that come from allowing Christ's attitude of kindness to reign in their hearts. If the two of you long for the shackles of wounded feelings to fall away, then we urge you to begin a personal pursuit of Christ. He is the key to changing you from feeling like cell mates to teammates.

An Ecclesiastes Marriage

The extreme importance we place on the need for a couple to be a strong *team* is taken from Ecclesiastes 4:9: "Two are better than one because they have a good return for their labor." Having had the advantage of laboring together nearly all of our married life, we long for couples to know the joy of working and succeeding together, even those whose lifestyles daily take them in different directions. So much more can be accomplished if the two assist each other in pulling the marital load.

To illustrate, consider the story of the horse-pulling contest we heard about. The runner-up horse managed 4,000 pounds, and the first-place winner hauled 4,500 pounds across the finish line. However, when the two horses were teamed they pulled an amazing 12,000 pounds of weight. This is a great picture of what can happen when both partners are fully involved in the marriage.

While the team effort described in Ecclesiastes 4:9 is of utmost importance, there are three additional advantages of marriage found in verses 10-12 of the passage. They are included in the verses of the song that has the three words we ask couples to sing with us.

I Need You

If there is work to be done
Two are better than one [vs. 9].
If there's a thief in the midst
One would be in peril
But two can resist [vs. 12].

And there're so many reasons
Why it will always be true
A man and a woman can say to each other
"I need you…oh, I need you."

If two hold hands when they walk
There's help if one of them falls [vs. 10].
And it's cold if you sleep alone
But two can lie down
And they will be warm [vs. 11].

And of all they can do for each other
The very best thing would be
Let God hold them together
There's greater strength in a cord of three [vs.12].

And there's so many reasons
Why it will always be true
A man and a woman
Can say to each other
"I need you…oh, I need you."[1]

Helping the other when he or she falls, finding warmth in companionship, and fighting the battles of life together are all incredibly wonderful by-products of making sure that the third cord, Christ Himself, is the focus of the teammates.

Using the biblical instruction of posting visible reminders of spiritual truth around our house (see Deuteronomy 6:6-9), there are three items in our kitchen that help us remember to keep the other's happiness as our first priority.

Years ago, after the Boones shared their life-changing wisdom with us, we wrote the following poem that a friend transcribed in calligraphy and framed for us. It says,

We believe a man and wife
Would have a better married life
If they would try out-serving one another
For deeper love is felt
When what is done is not for self
But when it's done to satisfy the other.

Along with that framed parchment, there is a two-ounce kitchen magnet that holds a ton of wisdom. It includes the following ideas on how to have a happy marriage. These brief suggestions taken from the face of our refrigerator have been slightly expanded.

1. Never be angry at the same time. Someone has to be calm. Remember, "a soft answer turns away wrath" (Proverbs 15:1 NKJV).

2. Never yell at each other—unless the house is on fire, then yelling is mandatory. "Death and life are in the power of the tongue, and those who love it will eat its fruit" (Proverbs 18:21).

   Yelling at one another is simply a form of "verbal shoving." When we use hurtful words toward one another we are attacking the very essence of our spouses. The old childhood adage "sticks and stones may break my bones, but words can never harm me" may be the biggest lie anyone every told. Sticks and stones can indeed hurt our bodies, and harmful words can negatively change who we are and how we look at ourselves.

3. If one of you has to win an argument, then let it be the other one. "Even a fool, when he keeps silent, is considered wise; when he closes his lips he is considered prudent" (Proverbs 17:28).

4. If you have to criticize, do it lovingly and sparingly. Remember, it might be your turn next time, so go easy. "The wise in heart will be called understanding, and sweetness of speech increases persuasiveness" (Proverbs 16:21). The test for whether or not something should be said is a threefold question: Is it true, is it kind, and is it necessary?

5. Never bring up mistakes of the past. Once they are dealt with, leave them alone. "[Love] does not take into account a wrong suffered" (1 Corinthians 13:5).

6. Never go to sleep with an argument unsettled. "Be angry, and yet do not sin; do not let the sun go down on your anger"

(Ephesians 4:26). Phyllis Diller says, "Never go to bed angry—stay up and fight." While it may be tempting to follow her advice, sometimes we should agree to finish discussing a matter the next day. Most of the time, hot emotion can cool after a night's rest and a solution can be achieved without hurt feelings.

7. At least once a day, try to say one kind or complimentary thing to your spouse. "Like apples of gold in settings of silver is a word spoken in right circumstance" (Proverbs 25:11). It shouldn't be too difficult for you to think of something nice to say. After all, your spouse was smart enough to marry you—that's reason enough to give a compliment.

8. When you have done something wrong, be ready to admit it and ask for forgiveness without making an excuse for the bad behavior. A confession without humility is bragging. "And forgive us our trespasses as we forgive those who trespass against us" (Matthew 6:13).

9. It takes two to make a quarrel, and the one who is in error is the one who usually does the most talking. Voltaire said, "A long dispute means both parties are wrong." (Was he married?) "When there are many words, transgression is unavoidable, but he who restrains his lips is wise" (Proverbs 10:19).

10. Neglect the whole world rather than each other. Amen!

The third item found in our kitchen that points us back to the joy of having one another as a teammate is the lyric to a song our daughter wrote for her husband, Emmitt Beall, prior to their wedding day. Even though Heidi penned these words, they accurately express how we feel to this day.

It's You

Never thought it could be so nice
Never thought it could be so wonderful
The first day we met, I knew right off the bat

We'd be together, oh, happily ever after,
It's you, it's you

Never thought it could be so nice
Never thought it could be so wonderful
To see you standing there, right beside me
Makes me wonder, just where would I be without you
Without you.[2]

three

A Partner, Not a Parent

We will never forget the elderly gentleman we met after a concert in Minnesota. We had just presented a musical look at the importance of family issues such as marital unity and devoted endurance to the promises made to one another. With a tone of confidence that belongs to those who have weathered the storms of life, he said, "I have a feeling you young folks would like to know how I've managed to get along with one woman for 57 years." Of course we took the bait, gave him our full attention, and waited for his gem of wisdom. He said, "Well…I don't try to run her life…and I don't try to run mine."

The mischievous twinkle in his eyes told us that we were allowed to laugh…and we did. And we've chuckled along with countless others as we've repeated the man's quip. However, not everyone responds with a smile to the levity. We've met husbands and wives who don't find it a laughing matter that their mates try to *run* their lives. No one gets married with the expectation of being bossed around and badgered by the very one who made forever promises to love, cherish, and honor. Yet, there are those who daily face living in insufferable situations where their opinion is not considered important nor their wishes valid.

What do people do when their beaus turn into bullies or their fair maidens turn into unfair manipulators? How does a spouse deal with the dilemma of being controlled and mistreated? To find relief, some have been known to take rather drastic measures. For example, consider the very tired wife and mother who decided to make her situation a matter of prayer. She begged God to "take care of" her husband. As you will see, it was a request that we're sure he was glad to see go unanswered! Perhaps you feel just as desperate and equally trapped as this woman. Listen to her story.

Annie: All alone, the woman sat in the back of the church. The rest of the 500 women who had attended the ladies' conference that weekend had already exited the auditorium. I was busy gathering up my books, papers, and props when I glanced toward the back of the building. That's when I saw her. Assuming she was there for a reason, I walked back to where she was sitting. Her head was bowed low and her shoulders were drooping. I quietly sat down in the pew in front of her. She then began to tell me her story.

She was the mother of three. Her oldest son, who suffered from muscular dystrophy, had been confined to a wheelchair most of his 17 years. Her athletic arms testified to the physical effort exerted as she lifted and carried her 150-pound son. Her other two children had a variety of learning and emotional challenges.

With her head bent she spoke in a soft whisper, "I'm married to a mean, hateful man who bullies me and tries to control every move I make. He makes my life miserable. He won't help me with our son, even refusing to pull the boy's underpants up while I hold him after he uses the bathroom." She went on to tell how she had buried her father that very week and had just learned the day before the conference that her father had disinherited her from his will. She said, "My dad hated my husband so much. He couldn't bear to think of his son-in-law enjoying anything he had worked for. That was my only hope of ever owning anything of my own. Now, I'm left to depend on my sister's generosity."

This sad woman then told me something that has haunted me from that day on. She said, "I came this weekend with one prayer. I was asking God to kill my husband. As mean and manipulative as he is to me, our children still love him, and I can't bear to take him away from them. Not too long ago I prayed, 'Dear Lord, I need a way out! I feel like a bird in a cage.'"

Embarrassed by her tears she finally lifted her eyes to mine and said, "Do you know what God said to me when I prayed that prayer? God spoke to me as clearly as I've ever sensed His voice and said, 'Even a bird in a cage sings.'"

With tears running down her face she asked, "What am I supposed to do with that? How do I live with that answer?"

Never having felt so utterly impotent, I replied, "If God says sing, then find your song." I offered some other words that were meant to encourage, but in the face of her deep pain and sorrow, even I could hear the hollowness of my words.

We parted. She went home to her difficult life, and I headed to a quiet hotel room. As I thought about this woman, I began to ponder, "Perhaps there really are people whose circumstances are so bleak that joy seems to be an absolute impossibility. How can she sing when she's so terribly sad?" Unfortunately, the answer to that question came too late for me to give it to the woman.

Sometime after meeting her, I was reading in Psalms, that great book in the Bible that offers balm and healing to the wounded soul. I came across the answer to her question, "How can a caged bird sing?" Psalm 9:9-12 speaks to the one who is hurting saying, "The LORD also will be a stronghold for the oppressed, a stronghold in times of trouble; and those who know Your name will put their trust in You, for you, O, LORD, have not forsaken those who seek You." It was the next verse that caught the eyes of my heart. "Sing praises to the LORD....He does not forget the cry of the afflicted."

Though I have not seen the woman since I met her, I long to tell her that God's Word is true, and it testifies to the faithfulness and attentiveness of God. In times of sorrow, God offers His grace to the afflicted. He alone must be her song. To worship Him is the reason she can sing while in a cage.

It is very possible that you, whether a husband or a wife, unfortunately find a certain level of camaraderie with the woman in that story. Your account may be different in that you may not have been driven to hope for the "death-do-us-part" portion of your wedding vows to come to pass. Yet, the outcome has been the same...you feel caged by control. Please be aware that you are not alone.

We asked couples to respond to an inquiry about the issue of control. We were quite amazed at the high percentage of husbands and wives (nearly 50 percent) who revealed their frustration in this area. We have included quite a few responses because of the enormous variety of "types of control." As you read the words of their hearts, do you find your

story among them? The actual question asked was: "Is your spouse a controlling type of person?"

Wives

* My husband was a psychology major in college. He uses his
  positive manipulation on me, and it drives me crazy. When he
  treats me like this, it makes me feel like a child. (Woman—
  married 11½ years—third marriage)

* He "needs" to make all the major decisions by himself. He
  expects me to go along with it. (Woman—married 34 years)

* My husband gets upset if I schedule anything on "his time." He
  wants my undivided attention, which means I can't talk on the
  phone to my friends if he's home. I feel suffocated by his
  demanding ways. (Woman—married 21 years)

* He controls me and everyone around him with his constant
  yelling. He acts displeased with any plans I make for us
  socially. (Woman—married 23 years)

* Sometimes I need for him to act controlling and jealous. I
  think this means he loves me. (Woman—married 9 years)

* He's passive/aggressive. I'm always trying to figure out how to
  please him without knowing what he wants. It's an impossible
  situation. (Woman—married 34 years)

* He tries to tell me how to do everything. He even tells me how
  to load the washing machine. I know his "control" is out of
  love. (Woman—married 48 years)

* He tries to control me by planning every little thing. He
  pouts and sulks when he doesn't get his way. (Woman—married 42 years)

* If I agree with my husband on everything, he is fine. If I don't,
  he thinks I don't love him or I want someone else. I just feel
  like when the kids are gone we will have nothing in
  common. (Woman—married 17 years—second marriage)

* He owns his own business and controls every aspect. He never shares with me. He says it's none of my concern. (Woman—married 13 years)

* He controls me by saying, "You're my wife, and you'll do what I say." (Woman—married 2½ years—second marriage)

* My husband is emotionally controlling. He makes me feel sorry for him, and I feel guilty because I'm not perfect and maybe I'm not always right about everything. (Woman— married 16 years—second marriage)

* He is an extreme controller. I am damaged emotionally because of the stranglehold he keeps on me and the way I think. (Woman—married 30 years)

* I have to carry a phone with me at all times so he can call me. If I don't answer immediately, he thinks I'm out cheating on him. I thought if I went along with his "need" to know it would make him feel secure. I feel badly for him, his dad cheated on his mom all the time, so I know where he's coming from. However, it's not gotten better, but worse. He has become more and more suspicious of me, without any reason whatsoever. We both are borderline insane, but it's gone on so long I don't ever see it getting any better. (Woman—married 22 years—five kids)

* My husband is slightly possessive, but two wives left him and he fears abandonment. (Woman—married 3½ years—second marriage)

* His control comes into play when he finds me tired and weak. Then he pushes to get his own way regarding purchases I'd not normally agree to. (Woman—married 39 years)

* The only way my husband tries to control me is his attempt to be the "helper" of the Holy Spirit in convicting me about areas he considers to be more important than I do. This behavior makes me feel childlike in our relationship. It is important to note here that there is a 16-year difference in our ages. Sometimes he treats me like his daughter instead of his wife. (Woman—married 16 years— second marriage)

* He controls all the money. The car, truck, house—everything is in his name. He doesn't want me to have friends or go anywhere. (Woman—married 35 years)

* Even though my husband is passive and most of the time I feel more like his mother than his wife, he still controls me by limiting the budget. He tells me no when I want to enroll in a computer class, for example. His behavior leaves me feeling tense and unfulfilled. (Woman—married 22 years)

* He tries to control things about my children. In a sense he makes me choose between the children and him. That's not fair. (Woman—married 9 months—second marriage—teenage children)

Husbands

* It's her way or nobody's happy around our house. (Husband—married 14 years—second marriage)

* Things need to go her way or she gets really moody. (Husband—married 30 years)

* Everything has to be done on her timetable regardless of what anyone else in the family has going on. It's all about her agenda. (Husband—married 19 years)

* My wife is very opinionated; it's almost scary. But to give her the benefit of the doubt, she always wants things done to help [get] things done for others, not just herself. (Husband—married 25 years)

* When things don't go smoothly, she gets really crazy. Her frustration level is pretty high when things don't go well. (Husband—married 12 years)

* My wife doesn't like to listen to suggestions and does her own thing. If things change, and she is not the one to initiate the change, then it upsets her. (Husband—married 7 years)

* My wife has to be in control at all times. She is very bossy! (Husband—married 10 years)

- Calling the shots! She has to be in control or everyone is miserable. (Husband—married 6 years—second marriage)

- My wife tends to be defensive and overly sensitive. She tends to be jealous if the kids seem to accept or like me more. (Husband—married 12 years)

- We both have control and trust issues and for good reason. We have no sexual relationship right now. We are in counseling for past sexual abuse in both our pasts. (Husband—married 5 years)

- My wife thinks I'm always comparing her to other women and looking at other women. I don't do that, and it's frustrating to be accused when I'm not guilty. (Husband—married 13 years)

- My wife is both controlling and jealous. She's working on it because she knows it's only hurting our relationship. (Husband—married 7 years—second marriage)

- If I don't give my wife 100 percent-plus of my time and attention, she gets upset and I live to regret the slight. She doesn't like for me to study my Bible and pray because it takes time away from her. She's really into watching things about the occult, witchcraft, and New Age stuff. She watches those shows on TV like *Sabrina* and *Charmed*. She wants me to watch them, too, and I don't feel it's right. She tries to control everything about my life, and if I am contrary to her—I really catch it! (Husband—married 4 years)

- My wife is very controlling. She says hurtful things in anger that she later regrets. (Husband—married 25 years)

- My wife expects me to do most of the housework and take care of the children. She wants her free time. (Husband—married 7 years)

- She doesn't try to control me as much as she bosses the kids around and uses anger to get them to listen to her. (Husband—married 21 years)

* She tries to control everything about me. (Husband—married 18 years—second marriage)

If the admissions of these husbands and wives ring a bell of familiarity in your heart, we have some helpful thoughts for you. Along with words of encouragement to those who are already in controlling, abusive marriages, we want to offer some instruction to newlywed couples to help avoid the same painful situation.

As we combed our questionnaires and read the responses, we realized that even though there are many forms that marital control and manipulation can take, all of the men and women seemed to express a single emotion. What are husbands and wives not telling each other?

"I need you to be my partner, not my parent. I feel suffocated and frustrated when you treat me like a child and boss me around. We can never truly love one another the way we need to until you are willing to treat me like an adult."

Help for the Controlled

We knew an elderly woman who told about her early years of marriage to her husband of some 50 years. She'd chosen to commit her life to a young man who had been raised in a horribly abusive situation where the father dictated every move the mother made. Her father-in-law's vise grip of control over his family was perverse to the extent that if his wife got pregnant and he didn't particularly want another child at that time, she was instructed to "get rid" of it. The young bride was very much aware of the sad little cemetery that was located on the backside of the in-law's property. It was the place where the tiny bodies of discarded babies were buried after they were aborted.

Knowing that her young husband had been reared in such a tyrannical environment, she was not surprised when, not long into their marriage, her husband's temper flared. In that moment she became acquainted with the back of his hand. As the roar of pain shot through her jaw, she immediately made a decision. She took a firm stance on their kitchen floor and said, "Today, you just hit me twice. The first and last time. Never again will you do this to me. If you do, I'm gone." He never raised a hand to her again.

While this woman understood her husband's upbringing and knew that he had a "built-in" weakness, she was not willing to allow him the kind of abusive control that he had learned in his earlier years from his dad. By "nipping it in the bud," she gave her young groom the very best wedding gift he could have ever received. Her resolute refusal to accept his raw, animal-like behavior motivated him to change his actions and reactions. Eventually he become the kindest man she had ever known. They went on to have a large family, and the cycle of abuse was broken. One determined woman, who refused to be controlled, changed a family's entire history.

Learning from this woman's courageous effort, we offer the following quote as a warning. If you are allowing yourself to be unreasonably controlled, consider the truth found in the book *Men Who Won't Lead and Women Who Won't Follow*, by author James Walker.

> If a wife allows her husband to dominate her, he comes to dislike her for being much less than a whole person. She is not his companion, nor his helper, nor his friend. She is simply his tool. Conversely, a wife who succeeds in gaining total influence over her husband will find herself living with a man she cannot respect. She can never be sure he loves her or just wants to minimize conflict. To win at the battle for control is, finally, to lose.[1]

It's a sobering thought that allowing ourselves to submit to such unkind treatment would have such unwelcome consequences. The parent/child type of relationship that results from such behavior is deadly to a marriage. If you see yourself as the one being unjustly ruled, perhaps the following suggestions will help you find a solution.

1. Discern the spirit of your spouse's attempt to gain control.

When we were first married, we moved into a huge farmhouse with two other couples. Because we were members of the "mid-1970s keep-it-simple, hippie club" and because our bell-bottoms' pockets were empty, we all shared the rental expenses. The cost of the house was $100 a month, which meant each couple had to contribute $33.33 to the rent fund. (Coming up with the extra penny at the end of each month wasn't always that easy. We took turns!)

Even though all the expenses were equally shared, the couple that had originally rented the house and signed the contract had the exclusive rights to serve in the role of domestic managers. Little did we realize, however, that when we moved in we had entered the domain of the "linen queen."

Our first indication that we were in trouble was when she demanded that we all fold the towels in one certain way. It was her way or else. She accepted no other form of folding and became quite upset when the rest of us didn't conform. One day a necessary rebellion took place. It was bound to happen. The verbal battle was fierce, and the word cannons roared with resistance to the "queen of woven cotton." The outcome was less than civil. Both towels and feelings were in a wad.

The point of this story is simple. There are some things that are just not important enough to make a big deal of. And when a person demands control over meaningless issues, he or she is revealing a spirit of pride and control that is unreasonable.

In the towel-folding situation, as well as in the everydayness of marriage, the best response is to not cave in to the demand. If you start giving in to unrealistic and unnecessary commands, you set yourself up for a lifetime of domination. Why? Behind that kind of manipulative attitude is a sinful spirit of pride and self-assertion that can never be fully satisfied. Again, as Barney Fife would say, it's time to "nip it, nip it, nip it in the bud!"

2. *Discern the* motive *of your spouse's attempt to gain control.*

A young wife told us of her husband's refusal to allow certain fashion magazines to be brought into their home. Her assessment of his request was that he was trying to unfairly control her reading habits. Feeling quite parented she said, "I'm near my mid-twenties, and I don't need to be made to feel like a child!"

Upon further inquiry, we learned that each time she opened the pages of the magazines and looked at the air-brushed, touched up bodies of the women in the pictures, she grew dissatisfied with her own appearance. When this happened, it affected her mood and ultimately her relationship with her husband. He saw this pattern and wanted to help her avoid it, thus, the reason for his request.

When the new bride realized that her husband had only her best interest in mind, she agreed to avoid those particular publications. The spirit of his stance on the matter was a worthy one, and she (and they) benefited by it.

Using this young couple's story as an example, there's a fine line between being *controlled* and being *cared for*. This is why it is so important for a husband and wife to make the effort to differentiate between the two. It requires asking some questions and being courageous enough to say and hear the answers.

3. Discern your reaction to your spouse's attempt to gain control.

Going back to the young couple and their magazine misunderstanding, when the newlywed wife was asked how she responded to the feelings that her husband's request was a parental attempt to restrict the entertainment found in the magazines, she said, "I pouted, stomped out of the room, and gave him a good dose of the silent treatment. I let him know that I hate it when he treats me like a little kid."

The next question asked of her seemed to cause her to quietly pause and give some thoughtful consideration to her reaction. She was asked, "How do you think a child would have responded?" Her humble reply revealed that the light had come on in her mind. "Only a child would have acted the way I did."

With that kind of answer, we knew there was hope for this young couple. Far too many wives, and husbands as well, would not be willing to face their error the way she did. Some wait much too long into their years of marriage to understand that if they want to be treated as an adult, they need to act like one.

Help for the Controller

When we put ourselves in the role of dominator over our spouses, we must realize the sad truth that the word *run* is only one letter short of becoming *ruin*. All you have to do is add the letter "i." Furthermore, when we seek to control, we make ourselves the enemy of our spouses. In a controller situation, someone has to lose.

The intent in the beginning of any marriage is not for one spouse to "beat up" the other with the club of control. Nonetheless, when mates are treated like children, they will eventually do what most children do who are ill-treated by a domineering parent. They will rebel and leave home. A sad ending to what was supposed to be a happy story.

Perhaps the one most to be pitied is not the controlled, but the controller. Those who feel like they are children living under the thumb of domineering mates deal with the feelings of frustration. On the other hand, those who desperately try to control their mates deal with something far more diabolical—fear. It is an anxiousness that has its roots in the sin of selfish pride. "I must have my way...because I'm always right" is their mantra as they tromp through the wounded hearts of those close by.

Ultimately, a controller lacks true love. If you find yourself on the parent side of the parent/child type of marriage, read the following section adapted from 1 Corinthians 13:4-5 and honestly answer the questions in the parenthesis. The scripture shows what love is.

Love is patient (are you?), love is kind (are you?)

And the passage shows what love is *not:*

Love is not jealous (are you?), love does not brag (do you?), love is not arrogant (are you?), it is not rude (are you?), is not self serving (are you?), is not easily angered (are you?), does not hold a grudge (do you?)

We strongly urge you, for the sake of your marriage, to hold yourself up to the light of these verses. If they reveal a characteristic you would like to change, it is not too late. As you prayerfully seek to be free from fear and to become a partner and not a parent to your mate, we encourage you to post the following passage on the wall of your heart and remember it daily: "There is no fear in love; but perfect love casts out fear" (1 John 4:18).

four

The Challenge of Change

Steve: It was the way Annie said, "Honey!" when she called for me that made me think that the word, "do," was not far behind. Sure enough, when I joined her at our front door she had that look on her face that was unmistakable. Something about the interior of our house was about to change. I just wasn't ready for the magnitude of it.

"Steve, don't you think this white entryway would look nice if it were a creamy yellow?" My heart sank like an anvil in a fishpond. Annie didn't understand that what I did *not* immediately imagine was the soft, springtime, pastel hue of a sun-filled entrance. Nor did I see, as she did, the expressions of pleasure that would lighten the faces of our guests who would step inside and experience some sort of spiritual epiphany as a result of the sight. Instead, my mind filled with the sound of clanging ladders, scaffolding being constructed, paint can lids popping free from their five gallon containers, and worse, the "cha-ching" sound of the hungry cash registers at our local hardware store.

In one brief moment and with one short sentence, I managed to make an attempt (my first and last) to dissuade my dear wife from such an enormous task. Using a tender tone of discouragement I said, "Annie, if it's yellow you want, why not wait? Time will do this job for us!"

With that pitiful effort at avoiding the ladder time that was ahead of me, I grabbed my truck keys and headed to the paint store. Needless to say, change did happen at our house.

And, I have to admit, it was indeed a very nice decor improvement...just like all the others I have resisted in the past.

That true story represents a couple of facts that are undeniable:

Women love change.

As proof of this unique female trait, husbands should take note of how often things seem to move around in their house when they're not looking. A picture that was on one shelf yesterday might be on another today. A piece of furniture that was in one corner last night somehow made a journey to the opposite corner this morning. For some fellows, it would be tough to survive as a blind man in their own home. Just ask our friend Charlie Norman, who lives in Texas.

Charlie retired to bed one evening and Carolyn, his wife, followed him there a few minutes later. Deep in the night they heard a noise in their yard. Charlie jumped out of bed and ran to look out of the living room window. As he jogged through the dark house, he met with an unexpected item that wasn't there just an hour or two earlier. Carolyn had moved the sewing machine! The result for Charlie was painful. He broke two toes that night, all because of a strange "nesting urge" that came over his wife just before she went to bed. "For some odd reason," he said, "she told me she just had to do it."

The second fact is:

Most men could go their entire lives and never change.

A lot of older guys, for example, have the same hairdo they had in high school—if they still have hair. And for some of our male friends of the '60s, it was Old Spice in the twelfth grade, and it's Old Spice today (probably the same bottle!). Most fellows could literally journey their whole course of time and be satisfied to have the same couch, kitchen table, and toothbrush. Perhaps the only change they care to make is a new truck. Of course, it'll be the same brand they drove as a teenager, just a newer model. The male trait of resisting change is proof that men are more like God than women. Why? Because of the passage in Hebrews 13:8 NKJV that says, "Jesus Christ is the same yesterday, today, and forever." (Please forgive us for this attempt at a little divine humor!)

In light of this observation, there is much truth to the saying that "a man will marry a woman hoping she never changes. A woman will marry a man with hopes that she can change him." Consequently, from the very beginning, men and women set themselves up for disappointment and conflict. We must confess, we have dealt with this dilemma just as many others have done.

Steve: When we married in 1975, my wardrobe consisted of one pair of blue jeans, two flannel shirts, and one well-seasoned pair of cowboy boots. Typical to males, I was very happy with my "get up." However, one day my flannel shirts mysteriously "got up" and left. I couldn't find them anywhere. When I looked in our closet, I found a new short-sleeve polo-style shirt. In one fell swoop I went from hippie to hip. When I asked Annie about my old, plaid, cotton friends, she announced, "They're gone!" That's all she said. So I braced myself for a trip to the pants section at the nearby discount mart.

Annie: When Steve and I dated and then married in the mid-1970s, my hairstyle was one length to my waist and parted in the middle. Many times he complimented me on my long locks and hinted from time to time that he hoped I would never cut them. As the 1980s were nearing a close, my hair was still one length to my waist and still parted in the middle.

Many hairstyles had come and gone during the nearly 20 years that had passed, but not mine! Though I was often tempted to sneak away and get a new and more easily managed look, I kept my "Crystal Gayle" hairdo for my darling. However, the urge to change became too much for me to resist. Finally, I brought it up to Steve. He threatened to shave his beard and blacken his white hair if I got mine cut and styled differently.

Believing (and hoping!) that he was bluffing, I headed to the beauty shop and the awaiting scissors. I was grateful for his reaction to the "new do" when I got home. He actually said he liked it but then added, "I love the new you, but please don't ever change again as long as we live!"

We are confident that many couples could tell the same kind of stories that we just told about dealing with the struggles brought on by change—or the lack of it. Though most spouses have had to make only minimal adjustments and concessions, as we did, some husbands and wives have encountered monumental conflict as they see their mates change...or not change. For these individuals, what they are hesitant to say to the other might be:

"I know we may have different expectations when it comes to change, but I must say, since we got married you've changed in some ways I didn't expect—and you haven't changed in the ways I expected."

Whichever of these statements you prefer to claim, one thing is always going to be true, (brace yourself fellows!)...change is inevitable. And the attitude with which we approach those changes will determine whether or not we survive the alterations that are sure to come. That attitude is flexibility.

Making the incredibly important decision to be bendable as a spouse is a key to your branch of the family tree not breaking *when* the winds of change begin to blow. Determining in advance to make the necessary adjustments will help your marriage survive.

Where Change Can Be Expected

When the areas of change that can occur are discussed with couples, we have discovered that the list can be long. For example, consider the physical changes brought on by time and gravity. One wife who was in her eighties said, "I have the same body parts I had at 20, they're just all in a different place!" A husband of 40 years said about his receding hairline, "Men don't lose their hair, it just goes underground and comes out their ears!"

Annie and I have not escaped the effects of time on our appearance. That fact came to light one day when we were traveling to a concert in a rental car...

> *Steve:* I'll never forget the afternoon we exited the Interstate and stopped at our favorite coffee spot...McDonald's. I went in and ordered two cups, and Annie waited for me in the car. When I returned I had exciting news. "Annie, you won't believe how cheap coffee is at this place. It was 61 cents total for both, can you believe it?"
>
> As I drove away I was still celebrating the great java deal. Annie was quiet as she stared at me. I could see her in my peripheral vision waiting for me to look at her. When I did, she mischievously said, "You don't know what just happened in there do you?"
>
> "What?" I asked in complete ignorance.

"They gave you the *senior discount!*"
I was devastated. Annie laughed. It was the first time anyone had ever openly implied that I was eligible for old-people's prices. I was tempted to turn around, go back to Mickey D's, find that young kid, and slap his jaws. However, I was so happy with the savings I quickly decided to let the boy live.

Because of the turning of the clock, each of us will face a host of physical revisions to our bodies. We should expect them so they don't surprise us. The truth is, as dreadful as things like squeaky joints and dentures in a glass might be, this area of change may be the easiest of all that we will face. Other changes are potentially more difficult. To name just a few, our lives can be altered by the loss of loved ones, having to move away from family and friends because of a job situation, emotional stress that goes along with caring for aging parents, and the uncertainty of retirement. All of these challenges require some thoughtful and careful advance preparation. However, we can say from experience that there is one change in a marriage that will affect a husband and wife more than all the others listed above.

Parenthood

Unless there is a medical reason or a predetermination not to bear children, most marrieds will likely face the incredibly life-altering role of parenthood. The woman will change in size and shape, and sometimes the man does as well. (*Annie:* Steve gained five pounds more than I did when I was carrying our first child. He said he was eating for three!) In addition, the woman will likely have hormonal reactions that tamper with her emotions and sometimes leave both her and her husband in tears...as they eat again.

We were a mere 15 months into our marriage when we learned that life as we knew it was going to change. We were gliding along through our world together, going wherever we wanted, keeping any hours we cared to keep, eating wherever and whenever we wanted to, and spending our dollars only on ourselves. Then...there was a necessary visit to the doctor. Eight months later, on March 20, 1977, our son was born. That day the passage found in 1 Corinthians 15:51 took on new meaning: "We shall not all sleep, but we all shall be changed (NKJV)."

That scripture was surely written for moms and dads with infants. Our happy-go-lucky lifestyle turned into a "Oh, no! He go stinky!" lifestyle. We, of course, fell in love with our little bundle of joy and would have never believed that poo-poo could smell like pudding. Boy, did we change…and often.

As wonderful as the difference was that our newborn (and eventually a second child, our daughter) had made in our lives, the years ahead would yield some challenges that would require an attitude of flexibility and maturity in order to survive.

Women seem to have less of a struggle with the entrance of a child into their lives. Perhaps a cause for this would be the enormous amount of undivided attention that they are more likely to give to their baby. Without realizing it, as the necessary care is being given to the infant, the changes that are simultaneously occurring in the marriage may be overlooked.

Men seem to have a harder time adjusting to the altered lifestyle, and the diminished amount of attention he receives from his wife is not always missed. The following dads were quite frank with their responses to a question we asked them. "How has having children changed your relationship with your wife?" Many of the answers show two emotions. Some dads reveal a sense of the delight found in Psalm 127:3-5 that declares, "Behold, children are a gift of the LORD, the fruit of the womb is a reward. Like arrows in the hand of a warrior, so are the children of one's youth. How blessed is the man whose quiver is full of them; they shall not be ashamed when they speak with their enemies in the gate." Other fathers honestly expressed their despair about the way that kids have affected their marriage.

Fathers

- At times the focus on the children has caused problems; however, they have taught us to pray together and, actually, we've grown closer to one another.

- Having children has deepened our love and mellowed our personalities. They have given us common goals.

- Children take too much of our time. They always come first. We've lost ourselves.

- Since we've had children, we have less sex. The more kids we have, the less sex there is.

- I miss the time we used to have together, and I miss the sleep I used to get. (Father of two—3 years old and 20 months old.)

- We have a blended family. She has two and I have two. It's really hard to mesh the two groups, but it's getting easier.

- I love watching her mother our children. I get to see more of her talents and personality. I'm really proud of her.

- I was present when our children were born. I don't think I'll ever get over watching her go through all she had to do to bring these children into the world. That experience has brought a closeness into our marriage that I didn't think possible.

- Our children have caused a problem between me and my wife. She doesn't want to do anything unless the children are a part of it. I feel left out and unimportant in her life.

- Seems like all we ever do are kid-related activities. I'd like to do something adult, just the two of us.

- We have conflicts in our marriage because we don't agree on how to handle situations with our kids, especially discipline.

- With kids we find it more difficult to find time to be alone with each other. Then when we are, we're both exhausted. It doesn't make for an exciting night of romance.

- As long as we have children in our home, we never lack sources of conversation. There's always something going on.

- Our children have enriched our lives and made us examine who we are. We started our relationship at 14, never dated anyone else, and married at 21. Although our time for each other is much less, our kids make us closer. I admire, love, and adore my wife even more since motherhood.

- Having children has made our marriage shallow and empty since we have no time for one another.

- When we had kids, my wife put me on the back burner. I went from #1 to #4.

- Knowing that if we were going to have any time alone we would have to "make it," we started going on short (and an occasional long) trips together. It's helped a lot.

- Most of our activities focus on the children. Other interests have been forsaken to support their activities. Sex is rare (maybe 2 to 4 times a year). She says the kids might hear or wake up...so we don't do it.

- She was always busy with the boys, and I was always busy with work. Now, she's busy with work, and I'm looking for time with my family. The sad things is, they're grown and gone.

- Children have strengthened our commitment to one another. We want to make our marriage work to provide a stable, intact home for our kids.

Fortunately for us, prior to having Nathan and Heidi, we were offered some wisdom about the potential for conflict that parenthood would have on our marriage. That insight came from a very reliable source—P.J. and Lillian Chapman (Steve's parents). They warned us that it would be a mistake to focus only on the kids: "If you're not careful to also tend to your roles as husband and wife, you could end up as strangers to one another by the time your nest is empty."

Because they had practiced what they had preached, we seriously considered their honest input. The following song resulted from their wisdom.

Who Are You?

Their hearts were broken as they told her goodbye
And they stood in the yard till she drove out of sight
Then they turned to face the first day and night
Of their last child leaving home.
She made some coffee, and he went outside
And all afternoon they never met eyes
And it was late in the evening when she realized
They hadn't spoken all day.

Then she looked at the photograph over their bed
Of the children she could say she knew
Then she looked at the stranger asleep in her bed
And she whispered, "Who are you?"

Years ago all they had was each other
They were best of friends and the best of lovers.
Then their good times made them father and mother
They did the job so well.
But lost in the details of raising the kids
Was a thing of most value that lovers can give
Keeping each other's needs at the top of the list
Of the things they've gotta do.

And he was the first to wake up the next morning
In a house that was quiet as a tomb
Then he looked at the stranger asleep in his bed
And whispered, "Who are you?"

But it's not too late for fathers and mothers
To go back to being best friends and lovers
It's sad when they whisper, "Who are you?"
Put each other's needs at the top of the list.
Do those lovin' things so easy to miss.
And don't forget to whisper, "I love you."[1]

Taking to heart the advice from the Chapmans served us well through the years. In order to avoid becoming strangers to each other, we consciously tried to be flexible enough to take breaks from our kids whenever the opportunities became available. Going out for lunch together, for example, while the kids were in school, asking a neighbor to spend a few minutes watching them while we took a walk, and even a few "day-cations" away from the kids were helpful. Again, being elastic was the key.

While we feel that we were successful at putting our marriage ahead of our parenthood, it was still very difficult to deal with another heart-wrenching aspect of being a mom and dad. "Letting go" of the kids introduced another reason for flexibility. Otherwise, the change would have been too excruciating. Those emotions are openly revealed in a song written after we talked to our friends, Ken and Donna Byrd, who live in Texas. Ken was preparing to drive his son to college, and their deep father/son connection made it even more difficult to think about the trip that he faced.

The Drive from Austin

He chose a school in Austin
Seems so far away.
I guess I should be happy
It's still in our state.
But if I had my way
He'd never leave the nest.
But we'll take him there tomorrow
Say goodbye and wish him the best.

I have rehearsed tomorrow
Every day for a year.
And every time I thought about it
I had to fight the tears.
But I'll be strong for him tomorrow
And tell him please come home often
But how I dread that drive back from Austin.

I think I'll come back on the two-lane
'Cause there's some sights I wanna see.
Some places south of Dallas
Where we made some memories.
But then again I might keep drivin'
To see that Corpus Christi moon
So I won't have to face tomorrow night
And his empty room.

I have rehearsed tomorrow
Every day for a year
And every time I talked about it
His mother walked away in tears.
But I'll be strong for him tomorrow
And tell him to please call home often.
But how I dread that drive back from Austin.

I should be crying for what the school is costin'
But that's not why I dread the drive back from Austin.[2]

Because Ken and Donna's son left home earlier than ours, there was no way we could fully feel the impact of the melancholy they were experiencing. But soon enough, we had our turn to understand their tears. Nathan had delayed going to college for two years after high school due to his work in the recording industry. While he did not live at home, he was close enough that it felt like he was still under our roof. When he did decide to go to a university in southern Tennessee, Heidi was only one year away from doing the same. Consequently, within 11 months, our house went from a center of teenage activity to a center for senior citizens. It was an "Ouch!" The following song describes the sudden realization that would require a level of flexibility we didn't expect to need.

Much Too Quiet

Where is the music that rattled the floor?
Where is the angry slam of the door?
Where are the questions "why" and "what for"?
It's much too quiet around here!

Where is the fighting that drove us mad?
Where are the conversations we had?
Where are the cries of happy and sad?
It's much too quiet around here!

How sweet is the sound of a child in the home.
Guess we assumed it would go on and on.
We never dreamed it would one day be gone,
It's much too quiet around here!

Oh!...love has a voice
And sometimes when it speaks
It sounds like a child makin' noise.

Where are the footsteps out in the hall?
The telephone hardly rings at all.
Your absence is noticed inside these walls.
It's much too quiet around here![3]

To say the least, the silence was deafening when our nest was finally empty. But Nathan reminded us of what a father of five children had said:

"Yes, they'll leave, but then they'll come back and bring a bunch with them!"

That memorable quip inspired our son to write the following response to "Much Too Quiet." We accepted his words as a fair warning!

Nathan's Response

You think it's quiet 'round here?
Just you wait till there's ten of us
A son and a daughter-in-law
With two kids each, climbing the walls.

Why do you worry about not hearing noise,
Screaming grandchildren will provide that joy.
They'll ask you questions and bang on the walls
More crying and ruckus than ever before.

Better write all your books and use all your paint,
Kids make it hard to concentrate.
You'll ask each other, "Why were we so sad,
When peace and quiet was here at our pad?"

The quiet you hear should be to warn,
It's only the calm before the storm.
Love has a voice that's been kind of loud
But I think love's getting ready to shout![4]

Yes, our kids have expressed their concern that we are now "all alone." Wondering if we were successfully weathering the winds of change, our married daughter, Heidi, called one day and asked, "Mom, are you and dad taking this empty nest thing O.K.?" Our response was, "Heidi, we got married to be alone! It just took us 25 years to get back to it. Yes, we're O.K.!"

While we are enjoying the return of the "it's just the two of us" years, there are friends our age who are dealing with still another change they didn't plan for as parents. These couples are living the story in the following lyric.

Making Room for Sarah

They made room for Sarah twenty-seven years ago
He gave up his office, she hung lace in the window.
They didn't mind the changes, they were glad to make the room,
And how the years flew by, and she was gone too soon.

Sarah met a man, and married when she was barely twenty-one.
They live in Virginia, with their only son.
But there's been some trouble, and she called today in tears.
Tonight there'll be some changes, 'cause after all these years

They're making room for Sarah, again.
She'll come home tomorrow; she'll be moving in.
They hope it all gets better, but they're not sure when.
They're making room for Sarah, again.

Some feelings are familiar, like that desk out in the hall
But should they leave the pictures of her family on the wall?
They hear the boy's a handful, and they pray they will be strong
But tonight they'll go to sleep, where it's been quiet for so long.

They're making room for Sarah, again.
She'll come home tomorrow; she'll be moving in.
They hope it all gets better, but they're not sure when.
They're making room for Sarah, again.

He'll fight the anger for the man, who's breaking his little girl's heart.
And she'll try to be her daughter's friend.
And let a little boy find comfort in his grandmother's arms.

They're making room for Sarah, again.
She'll come home tomorrow; she'll be moving in.
They hope it all gets better, but they're not sure when
They're making room for Sarah again. [5]

Those who are doing well in the midst of this unexpected alteration of their lives have been able to do so because of their willingness to be flexible. Kids do come, leave, and even sometimes return. In light of this truth, we hope those who are parents and preparents will be encouraged to expect changes and to prepare for them. Perhaps by knowing these things in advance, you will deal more successfully with the years ahead.

The Pages Turn

My life is like a story written down in time
With fewer words before me
than there are behind.
Once a child, I now have children
Who have children of their own.
I wish I could be with them
But there's a reason I'm alone.

'Cause the pages turn,
The chapters close.
Line by line
The story goes.
How quick it reads
As the candle burns.
The years go by
And the pages turn.

I face it at reunions with names I can't recall.
I see it in old pictures hanging on my wall.
And I hear it in old love songs
That draw me somewhere to my past.
My book is in the hands of time,
And he's reading much too fast.

And the pages turn.[6]

five

Connected or Co-Naked

One of our most favorite quips about sex came from a man who was nearing 60 years of age. Someone asked him, "Is there sex after 50?" He responded, "Oh, yes, and I especially enjoy the one in the spring!"

While it may be true that the frequency of marital intimacy may wane as we approach our later years, its importance seems to endure. And the level of satisfaction in the area of sex often has a bearing on its significance to a spouse. This is expressed in the well-known adage that says, "If sex is good, it's only 10 percent important...if it's bad, it's 90 percent important."

As a result of speaking and singing at many weekend events designed for married couples, we often have the opportunity to observe an interesting phenomenon in regard to the expectations of husbands and wives. As the couples gather and register on the first evening, there is a sense of anticipation on the faces of both the men and the women. While we rejoice that each spouse seems happy to be present, we know that more than likely, they each have their own unique reasons to be excited. Most of the women have arrived with hopes that the weekend will result in a deeper connectedness. Many of the men, on the other hand, are just hoping for more co-nakedness.

We admit that this male/female difference is not true for every husband and wife who attends our seminars. Yet both hopes are valid. To bridge the gap that exists between being connected and co-naked, a healthy compromise must be reached. The husband would do well to accept his wife's need for him to be "emotionally naked" so that he can hear her heart. Conversely, the wife needs to be willing to accept her husband's need for her to be physically naked in order to meet his needs. The result will please both husband and wife. So what do husbands and wives need to say to each other?

> "Somehow, we've got to find a bridge between the wife's need to be connected and the husband's need to be co-naked. As a wife, I need you to be willing to be emotionally naked before me, so that I can feel connected to you. As a husband, I need you to be willing to be physically naked before me, and meet my sexual needs, in order for me to feel connected to you."

In order for a couple to achieve this sexual balance in marriage, truthful communication about this issue is paramount. Perhaps one of the most tragic results of two people failing to talk honestly is found in one of the questionnaires we received from a wife. She wrote, "I didn't marry until I was in my early thirties, and I married a man 15 years older than me. He had diabetes and a lot more problems than I realized. The wedding night was a disaster because it was that night that I found out he was impotent due to his diabetes."

How incredibly cruel it was for this man to withhold such pertinent information about his health. His silence robbed her of the information she needed to make an informed decision about committing to him in marriage. Of course, this is an extreme example of the harm that remaining silent can do to a couple. Yet communicating clearly should happen, even though most of us might have less dramatic information to share. To do so might bring about some needed healing and wholeness to relationships.

We are very much aware, by the way, that to bring up the word "communication" will cause some fellows to want to turn off their hearing aids. However, to help the guys appreciate the need to converse with their wives about this subject, we go to the wit of one half of the popular author and speaking team, Chuck and Barb Snyder. Chuck says, "Communication is kind of like vomiting...you don't want to do it but it feels good when you get it over with!"

With that, we offer the following communication from several husbands and wives who have "brought up" some things they have yet to
tell their spouses. Perhaps their willingness to be honest will encourage
you to do the same. First, wives were asked to complete this sentence,
"In regards to sex, if I could, I would tell my husband to *stop...*"

- wanting sex every night.

- turning me down when I want sex.

- talking about sex and just love me.

- thinking I want sex all the time.

- being so tired, overworking, and using all your energy up
  before you get to me.

- getting up after sex and leaving me alone in the bedroom.

- criticizing me and my ability to satisfy him.

- asking me to "do it" in the afternoon when the kids are
  around.

- being so rough.

- looking at pornography. It makes me feel dirty when he looks
  at me after he's watched that filth.

- wanting to "play" at 10:30 at night when I'm exhausted.

- trying to change me.

- wanting sex in the morning before I'm ready to get up.

- womanizing and committing adultery.

- going to sleep so quickly.

- expecting things I don't want to do.

- waiting until 5 minutes before we go to bed to recognize I'm a
  beautiful, desirable woman.

- making sex my job, instead of a romantic connection.

- treating me with harshness and anger when I say no.

- making me play fantasy games and making up stories.

The wives were also asked to complete this sentence, "I would tell my husband to *start*...."

- enjoying me for who I am and allow me to say no when I don't want to have sex.

- touching, hand-holding, caressing me just because he loves me, not as a precursor to sex.

- treating me special, not like a porn queen.

- cuddle more.

- initiating more sex.

- giving more compliments and nonsexual affection.

- being more loving and affectionate on the days he doesn't want sex.

- hugging and talking more.

- giving more time for hugs and kisses leading up to sex.

- coming to bed earlier.

- spending time to make me feel like it's me he wants, instead of focusing on having his needs met.

- working harder on fresh breath and a cleaner body.

- treat me like a human with feelings instead of using sex as a weapon on me.

- remember what I like and don't like.

- relaxing more and enjoying being with me; don't be in such a hurry.

- taking care of his body, eating right, and attending to his health.

- being more aggressive and romantic.

- telling me he loves me, rather than assuming I know it.

- talking to me and showing an interest in what I think is important.

- holding me, kissing me, touching me without worrying about whether he will be able to reach orgasm or not.

While the women were very willing to share their thoughts, the men were a bit less eager to do the same. Regardless of the inhibited and abbreviated nature of their answers, the men responded by completing the same sentences.

"If I could, I'd tell my wife to *stop*..."

- worrying about other people in the house.

- getting up and leaving me all alone afterward.

- punishing me. I could never tell her to stop, she'd punish me for a long time if I tried to be contrary to her.

- thinking of our sexual relationship as a job.

- talking herself out of the mood.

- taking me for granted.

- I don't tell her to stop!

- always being tired.

- saying "no" so much.

- being so busy.

- procrastinating about her physical problems.

- being shy about her body.

- being so closed-minded about various sexual activities.

- falling asleep.

- just thinking it's a responsibility.

- feeling that it's a bad thing.

- thinking or talking about other things during sex.

- being stressed.

"I would tell my wife to *start*..."

- being more aggressive [this was the most common comment].

- initiating the lovemaking. I need to know she wants me.

- being in a better mood.

- enjoying sex.

- being more spontaneous [also a very common comment].

- being more playful and having a good time.

- telling what she wants and what she enjoys....I want us to connect more physically and relationally.

- losing weight.

- focusing on my needs and feelings more.

- taking more of an interest in our sexual relationship.

- making more time for us; put "us" on her priority list.

- getting her sex drive back.

- showing more affection to me.

- kissing me more.

- becoming more of a participant rather than just lying there uninvolved.

- making time for us instead of centering on everyone else.

- initiating lovemaking because she wants to be with me, not just because she thinks I want to do it. I can tell when her heart is not in it.

- to do anything! She has a medical problem that takes away all of her sex drive.

Perhaps as you perused these very candid statements, one of them sounded a tone of familiarity in your heart. If so, we encourage you to prayerfully seek an opportunity to discuss it with your mate. *Communication* will indeed contribute to the joy of being both *connected* and *co-naked*. But as they say in the TV infomercials, "But wait! There's more..."

Commitment: The Cornerstone to Sexual Fulfillment

All of us know that any two people can have sex, but not every couple knows true intimacy. For example, a man who hires a prostitute for an hour is not being intimate with her when they engage in the physical act. In no way will he *know* her as 1 Peter 3:7 commands. That passage instructs a husband to live with his wife "in an understanding way." Fulfilling this command requires time, attention, and...*commitment*.

A woman who invites a man into her chambers for the purpose of offering herself free of charge is also a woman who will not know true intimacy. Instead, she is assisting him in avoiding the one thing that could help her know real oneness...*commitment*. Why does an exclusive devotion to one person bring about the closeness that husbands and wives desire? For the answer to that question, it is best to go to God's Word.

In Matthew 19:4-6, Jesus responded to some Pharisees who were testing Him about whether or not it was permissible to divorce for any reason:

> And He answered and said, "Have you not read that He who created them from the beginning made them male and female, and said, 'For this reason a man shall leave his father and mother, and be joined to his wife, and the two shall become one flesh?' So they are no longer two, but one flesh. What therefore God has joined together, let no man separate."

Essentially, true marital oneness is a result of obeying God's command to join together. Only in the holy ground of obedience can oneness grow. For that reason, we want to look at four areas of commitment to our spouses that can yield the sweet fruit of intimacy, the kind of spiritual oneness that results in physical fulfillment!

Commit to Stay

In 1975, Steve and I stood at the front of a little country church in West Virginia and made some serious promises to each other. Through the years, the obedience to being faithful to those vows has contributed as much as anything to creating the fertile soil where love's roots can grow deep. We both determined that day in 1975 that neither the termites of differences nor the tornadoes of trouble would topple our family tree. Our resolve to stay true to our covenant commitment was described in this lyric using a maritime metaphor.

The Ships Are Burning

We made this journey
We sailed here together
We made a promise
We'd stay here forever.

But when we reached the shore
We kissed the ground
You took my hand
And we turned around
And we smiled while we watched the flames
Light up the night.

'Cause the ships are burning
There'll be no turning back
For you and me
Whatever we find here
We've made it clear
Here is where we'll always be.

And on this island of pleasure
There'll be some dangers
And we might think about returning
But we both know
We won't go
That's why…
The ships are burning.

But too many lovers are
Keeping their ships anchored in the bay
And one by lonely one
We've seen them sail away.

But when we reached the shore
We kissed the ground
You took my hand
And we turned around
And we smiled while we watched the flames
Light up the night.

'Cause the ships are burning
There'll be no turning back
For you and me
Whatever we find here
We've made it clear
Here is where we'll always be.

And on this island of pleasure
There'll be some dangers
And we might think about returning
But we both know
We won't go
That's why...
The ships are burning.[1]

We encourage you to take a few minutes to either read this lyric to each other, or write down in your own words your pledge to stay with your spouse. In some way, reassure him or her of your commitment and that leaving is not an option. The peace and confidence that will result from this renewal can once again launch you to true passion.

Commit to Purity

Adultery is sin, and sin never unites. Like a wedge of iron, it always divides. And of all the casualties that adultery causes in a relationship, intimacy could very well be its first victim. But there is hope. While the pleasure of "another lover" might be a fierce temptation, it *can* be avoided. How? One thing that can motivate a spouse who is being "drawn aside" by someone else is to carefully consider the price that has to be paid for the pleasure of another.

A great picture of the deadly cost of adultery is found in a hunting story.

(*Annie:* Ladies, bear with Steve as he tells this true tale. It's about a wild turkey, and it will help to remember that...it takes one to hunt one! Seriously, this is a good story.)

Steve: I sat at the edge of a beautiful green field on an April Tennessee morning waiting for the sun to come up. I was hoping to see some turkeys, especially an old male gobbler. Not long after dawn I looked across the 200-yard field and saw two dark forms exiting the woods. My heart raced when I realized they were turkeys, and one of them looked like he might be a legal bearded male.

As the hen fed on the insects and tender grasses, she slowly meandered toward me. The male wasn't much interested in the food at his feet. Instead, the springtime mating season caused him to be totally focused on the hen, which meant wherever she went, he followed.

Consequently, he, too, was gradually moving toward the end of my gun barrel.

Knowing that any quick movement would alert the highly skilled eyes of the birds, I remained motionless, trusting my camo clothes to conceal me. I kept my shotgun resting on my knee in position to shoot. Finally the pair wandered to within about 70 yards of me, and I could clearly see the 10- to 11-inch beard that the "tom" sported. With nerves that wanted to wobble like Jell-O, I very slowly curled my index finger around the trigger guard and quietly slid the safety to the off position. Not wanting to risk a shot more than 40 yards for fear of only wounding the bird, I waited for the two birds to close the distance gap. However, something went wrong.

As if the hen had found the epicenter of tasty grasses, she "hung up" out at the 70-yard mark. Naturally, the male did, too. As his love interest pecked the ground for her breakfast, he fanned his tail feathers and did his ceremonial strutting. It's an unusual ritual to see, to say the least. Around in circles he went, back and forth, round and round again. As I watched and waited, I had to wonder what the human equivalent would be for the turkey's strange attempt to impress a girl. I suppose it would look like a body-building competition contestant who has gone through his muscle display program then steps to mid-stage and takes that final, fully pumped stance, the one that makes it look like their facial veins are about to explode leaving oil-coated skin shrapnel on the front row of the screaming audience. With that totally tense pose, then he would walk in circles around a female...all morning for about an hour. (I am so glad that human males don't have to do this as a part of the mating ceremony! A rose and a hamburger is all a fellow needs.)

After about ten minutes of waiting for the hen to lead her beau closer to my weapon, I grew impatient. As she fed and he acted like a fool, I very slowly reached into my waist bag and took out one of my turkey calls. It was a long slender wooden box with a flat, sliding cut of wood mounted to it. I wanted the gobbler to think I was back in the woods a bit so I gingerly slid the flat piece of wood across the top of the box. The sound it made was supposed to be the voice of a hen saying, "Hey, big boy, I see you out there in all your glory! Come to me, darlin'!"

I've hunted turkeys long enough to know that if the "tom" would drop out of strut, look my way, and even gobble at the sound of my call, he would probably be interested enough to leave his hen and head toward the other girl. As I softly simulated the call of another hen, I was sure he would like the sound. I was confident of this because it even made me excited. However, the old bird never gave me a moment's notice. He remained completely focused on the hen he was circling. I tried the box call again. Nothing happened.

I took out a second type of call. It was a slate plate about the size of the bottom of a large coffee cup and a wooden stick (called a "striker") that looks sort of like a pencil. I gingerly scraped the striker across the plate making a "purring" sound. It is the noise turkeys often make when they're browsing for food. It's the sound of calm and happy. I wanted the gobbler to think that not only was the other hen nearby a real "looker," she also had a sweet personality. Nothing happened. Not even once did he look my way.

Frustrated and afraid I was about to lose the birds to the far side of the field, I finally reached into my bag, took out my guitar, and started singing, "Have I told you lately that I love you?" Well, I didn't have my guitar along, but the idea crossed my mind!

The outcome of that morning hunt does not fall in favor of the human. That old gobbler never did look in my direction, and eventually he wandered off with that smart hen he was with. And you're wondering by now what the point of this story is? It should be obvious, but I'll tell you anyway.

Had that old male turkey given attention to "the other hen" who was calling for him, and if he would have moved to within range of my shotgun, he would have paid a terrible price. However, because he remained faithful to the one he was with, he's still alive. What a clear picture of the importance of a man staying true to his wife. The price a husband has to pay for the sin of adultery is far too great.

The following lyric was written to list some of the costly treasures that a man should never be willing to pay for another woman.

What I Wouldn't Give

She gave that signal, she had that walk
Something inside me began to talk.
"Ain't she fine." I said, "I agree."
I felt the danger when she looked at me.

I started wondering how she would feel
I started thinking how I might close the deal
I could say I didn't, when, I really did
If I could have her, what I wouldn't give
Oh, what I wouldn't give...

My wife, her smile, our memories, the miles
Our children, their trust
And everything that God has given us
That's what I wouldn't give
For her.

It's not the first time, and there'll be more
There's a million battles in this—one war
But God knows, I want to win
What I wouldn't give for her, let me say it again.

My wife, her smile, our memories, the miles
Our children, their trust
And everything that God has given us
That's what I wouldn't give
For her.[2]

Annie: Steve's song lyric is not only applicable to men; women should also be unwilling to pay the cost of adultery. A pastor shared the sad account of five women in his congregation who had left their husbands and families for lovers they met on the Internet. The foolish choices these women made illustrate the fact that adultery is not a gender issue. It's a matter of sin.

Referring once again to the danger of responding to the call of "another," it must be stated that the enticing voices that can be heard are not always in the flesh. Sometimes the call comes from forms on the pages of magazines, images on a computer monitor, and figures moving on film. Committing to purity includes saying no to the vast opportunities offered by the world around us to stray from our mates. That determination might be inspired by a poem we once read...

All the water in the world
However hard it tried
Could never sink a ship
Unless it got inside.

All the evil in the world
The wickedness and sin
Can never sink the soul's craft
Unless it gets within.
—*Author unknown*

The scriptural encouragement we offer as a help to husbands and wives who need a reason to say a firm no to the other voices is found in Hebrews 13:4: "Marriage is to be held in honor among all, and the marriage bed is to be undefiled; for fornicators and adulterers God will judge." This verse should wake the souls of wandering spouses from their "death wish" for their marriages!

In addition to the sobering verse in Hebrews, we suggest that a couple do the following two activities in order to cultivate accountability to each other in regard to sexual temptation. First, as soon as the time can be taken to do it, read Proverbs 7 together and study the text. Take note especially of verse 23 that offers insight into the result of following the path of adultery to its end: "He did not know it would cost his life" (NKJV).

The second suggestion requires a daily commitment to communicate a specific statement to each other. The following lyric reveals what to say and when to say it. The seasoned and successful couple who lived this true story provide a wonderful role model for us all.

Faithful to You

Thirty years ago, one night in May
He came home from work in a strangely quiet way
And just before they closed their eyes and drifted off to rest
He turned to her and whispered, "I must confess."

"You know a salesman's life is a lot of time alone.
Today I made a call, 'bout sixty miles from home
And there was a woman, with a look in her eyes
And the thought that crossed my mind, took me by surprise."

"But I can end this day, with peace in my heart
Though I was away, and we were miles apart
I can come back home, and tell you that it's true
Today, I've been faithful, faithful to you."

And so they made a promise, and sealed it with their tears
That all their days would end like this, they've kept it though the years.
And it's helped them in those moments, when love was put to test
To know that night they'd face each other
And from their hearts, confess

"I can end this day, with peace in my heart
Though I was away, and we were miles apart
I can come back home and tell you that it's true
Today, I've been faithful, faithful to you
I'll always be faithful, faithful to you."[3]

It's not enough to promise to stay and fight the battle. While these resolves are imperative to gaining the truest of intimacy, there's another aspect of commitment to consider.

Committed to Satisfy

Nothing could be more clear about the need for a couple to be mutually concerned with meeting the sexual needs of their spouses than the passage in 1 Corinthians 7:3-5. In regard to marital sex, the scripture instructs:

> The husband must fulfill his duty to his wife, and likewise also the wife to her husband. The wife does not have authority over her own body, but the husband does; and likewise also the husband does not have authority over his own body, but the wife does. Stop depriving one another, except by agreement for a time, so that you may devote yourselves to prayer, and come together again so that Satan will not tempt you because of your lack of self-control.

The word *duty* in the opening line of the passage is not meant to imply that sex is merely another job, a dreaded task, or a necessary evil. Instead, the meaning in the original language gives a much more attractive perspective to physical relations. It is taken from the Greek word *eunoia*, which means to favor the other in the mind or to think about a spouse with affection. The scripture also instructs that fulfilling your spouse's sexual needs is not optional, but it is an opportunity to meet a need in your mate that no other human being can righteously fulfill.

Annie: I want to offer a word of encouragement to the young wife who feels guilty when she reads the 1 Corinthians passage. Perhaps the demands of your life has resulted in a lengthy "to do" list. Unfortunately, your husband's name is either very near the bottom or not on it at all. If this is true, please keep in mind that the "back burner" was made for cooking, not for him. Proverbs 14:1 strongly warns, "The wise woman builds her house, but the foolish tears it down with her own hands." Please take to heart the scripture's advice that says your husband's sexual needs are not only your responsibility, but also your privilege.

Steve: In a desire to come to the aid of the tired and frazzled wife who may wince at what Annie just advised, I offer two tips to husbands. The first is embodied in a lyric I wrote after I heard Annie confess one day that there are times when her workload makes her feel like nothing more than a machine, like something inhuman made of metal. She admitted that there were times when she simply needed to be held so that the reality of being a real person could return. Thus the song...

Metal

Sometimes I feel, like I'm made of steel
An assembly line machine, just grinding out the days
Sometimes I confess, I need to feel like flesh
And let the metal fall away.

So, baby, won't you hold me tonight.
Darling, won't you hold me warm and tight.
Touch my hand, feel like flesh again
And let the metal fall away.

Sometimes I fear, the words I hear
Coming from my lips, that only cold and hard could say.
But, baby if you will, break through the steel
And help me let the metal fall away.

So, baby, won't you hold me tonight.
Darling, won't you hold me warm and tight.
Touch my hand, feel like flesh again
And help me let the metal fall away.[4]

The second tip I offer comes again from my love of the great outdoors. "Good hunters make good lovers!" Let me explain. I enjoy every aspect of hunting the whitetail deer. I like, for example, choosing the right pattern of camouflage clothes to wear. If the leaves are fallen and the woods are filled with bright sunshine, I'll wear a lighter color of camo. If the foliage is still on and the woods are filled with shadows, I wear a darker color.

I also enjoy finding where the deer are moving, or, as most hunters call it, scouting. This necessary part of the pursuit takes me to places such as thickets where I can observe signs of the whitetail's presence such as bedding impressions, droppings, scrapes, rubs, and subtle trails.

Scouting also leads me to study the animal's crossing points along fence lines. A lot can be learned about the kind of animals that are traveling through the area, the directions they prefer, and the frequency of use. A strand of barbed-wire can reveal the hair left behind from all sorts of critters like deer, bear, and old hippies.

By now you may be asking, "What on earth does this have to do with a man being a good lover?" Here's the deal, to put it as tactfully as I know how, a good hunter will make a good lover because he cherishes every detail of the pursuit...not just pulling the trigger! If all he cares about is the "shot," he is nothing more than a killer.

Do you get the point of this analogy? Points (antler) are important to deer hunters, and this point is really vital if you as a husband want to help your wife not feel like you are just another item on her "to do" list. The old saying "sex begins in the kitchen" really is true. A man would be wise to make it his priority to serve his wife outside of the bedroom if he expects her to be amicable inside the bedroom.

Being committed to satisfy her, and her alone, should be your highest pursuit as a husband. Your unwavering devotion to meeting only her needs will be a blessing to your wife, and, to be sure, it has great rewards. Consider this passage from Proverbs 5:15-21.

> Drink water from your own cistern and fresh water from your own well.
>
> Should your springs be dispersed abroad, streams of water in the streets?
>
> Let them be yours alone and not for strangers with you. Let your fountain be blessed, and rejoice in the wife of your youth.

As a loving hind and a graceful doe, let her breasts satisfy
you at all times; be exhilarated always with her love.

For why should you, my son, be exhilarated with an adul-
teress, and embrace the bosom of a foreigner?

For the ways of a man are before the eyes of the LORD, and
He watches all his paths.

I personally love this promise God has given to husbands who do not
run to the door of a "foreign" woman. That our wives can be our sole
sources of satisfaction is indeed exciting. And, may I admit as a
hunter/lover, I love God's usage of the deer analogy, that is, the "hind
and the doe" breast thing.

Words That Heal

Since this book is about the importance of husbands and wives
saying things to each other that can restore health to a marriage, we offer
you the opportunity to read together the following poem. As you take
a quiet moment, use these words as a healing salve on the hearts of flesh
that have been scraped by the metal of life's demands.

You Take My Breath Away

How I love your hair
And the way you stare at me,
It takes my breath away.
How I love your smile,
You drive me wild
You take my breath away.

I can't remember cold with you to hold
You are my fire.
Warm and safe right here
With you so near
You take my breath away.

Flesh and bone will die
And the tears will dry
I long to be there
Time will take away
The joy and the pain,
And take my breath away.

Stay with me, please don't leave
'Cause you would take my breath away
Life, joy, pain, they're all the same
But you take my breath away.[5]

six

I Need a Friend

Mary Williams was a neighbor who, at the time of our little family's arrival to her street, had been a widow for nearly 20 years. We all grew to love her, and she especially enjoyed the company of our two little kids (except for the day they delivered the bouquet of freshly picked flowers...from her own garden!).

Mary occasionally admitted her feelings of loneliness to us. Perhaps the most heartbreaking statement she made was, "I just miss having someone to 'what if' with." When we asked her what she meant, she said with a reflective smile, "Well...after our son and daughter grew up and left home, and it was just the two of us, I found great joy in saying from time to time, 'John, *what if* we go see my sister today?' or, 'John, *what if* we go to Morrison's Cafeteria today for lunch?'"

Mary then paused and fought the tears away, then went on to a different subject. However, her honest wish for having her husband back never left our memories. We took it as our cue to treasure the time together that God has given us.

It is very easy to overlook the value of what Mary was describing when she talked about "what-if-ing" with John. Basically, she longed for her best friend. And she's not the only one. Many others, including widowers and single-again individuals, struggle with feeling alone in the world. But of all those who may be lonely, none seem to be more emotionally isolated than the married man or woman who feels dis-connected from the friendship of a mate. Consider this lyric.

The Loneliest One

The loneliest one in this town tonight
Is not the one who's alone when they turn out the light
It's the one who stares in the dark at the end of the day
Lying next to the one who feels so far away

The bed is warm
But the heart is cold
Not a word said
But the story is told
Where two people lay and one of them cries
Is the loneliest one in this town tonight.

Somebody once told me
These words are so true
Lonely is love if it's only you
And the saddest place on this earth is still
In arms that are empty that long to be filled.[1]

If this lyric describes your marriage, we encourage you to recognize an important progression that may have taken place in your lives as a couple. It's a flip-flop that seems to happen to far too many husbands and wives. When they are dating, their focus is completely on the other person, and they seem to have little trouble finding friend-type things to do that are fun and memorable. However, after they are married it doesn't take long before a mountain of responsibility hides their view of the value of friendship. Those unforgettable things they enjoyed doing before the wedding often are buried under the heap of cares. To illustrate this fact, look at the answers some husbands and wives gave to the fol-lowing question: "What do you and your spouse do for fun?"

Wives

* Nothing I can think of. (Married 12 years)
* Not much of anything. (Married 6 months)
* It's been so long since we had fun together I forget. (Married 14 years—second marriage)

Husbands

- Nothing. (Married 10 years)
- Watch TV. (Married 16 years)
- We work together; we're too busy to do other stuff. (Married 12 years)

These few responses represent a host of similar comments about the absence of fun in married relationships. In fact, when the respondents got to that particular question, many of them simply left the space blank. The unspoken cry many of these husbands and wives left off the paper might be worded best in this way:

> "Yes, I need for you to be my lover, but I also need a friend! I miss having fun with you."

F-R-I-E-N-D-S-H-I-P

For the purpose of helping you return to the joy of "what-if-ing," perhaps the following acrostic of the word *friendship* will be useful in rediscovering some aspects of being friends that will renew this very important part of your relationship.

F—Find Fun Things to Do Together

Someone once said, "Friendship is like a bank account. You can't continue to draw on it without deposits." Drawing from some of the husbands and wives who responded to our question about the things they do together for fun, here are some unusual ideas.

- We took dance classes together. I have two left feet but she doesn't seem to mind because she still has two feet left!
- We take showers together. (Clean is not all you might get!)
- We picnic in the park, or sometimes we park in the picnic area.
- We often take walks in the evening after dinner and talk about our day and what's going on in our lives. We also talk about our kids and fight the temptation to keep walking, and walking, and walking...
- We diet together at Pizza Hut.

- We juice together (you know, carrot juice, apple!).

- When we get bored we play a board game until we get bored.

- We love to go to our local hardware supercenter and walk around and dream. We don't usually wake up until we get home.

Steve: While fun is most often found outside the home, away from kids, phones, and dishes, sometimes good times together can be enjoyed within the walls of the house. I'll never forget the note Annie wrote to me. I found it on the front seat of my truck, but I didn't discover it until I was a few miles down the road. It simply said, "For a good time, call home!" Shucks, I did the smart thing. I saved my cell phone pennies and turned around and went back to the house!

A friend of mine, Zane Carson, gave me the idea for the following lyric. I was talking to him one evening, and he told me he had the next day off from work. I asked him what he had planned to do. What he told me is a great idea for any husband who wants to make a memory with his wife/friend. Plus, I like Zane's idea because it doesn't cost a thing and no travel is involved.

Bother My Baby

I don't have to work tomorrow
I wonder what I'll do,
Maybe I'll go fishin'
With a friend or two.
There's at least a thousand places
And faces I'd like to see,
But the best idea I've ever had
Just occurred to me.

I think I'll stay home
And bother my baby.
I think I'll stay home
And get in her hair.
I think I'll stay home
And bother my baby.
And maybe if I stay home
I'll get somewhere.

I'll follow her into the kitchen
Just to see the way she walks.
I'll call her on the other line
Just to hear her talk.
I'll go outside and ring the doorbell
Just to hear her say, "Come on in."
I'll play a little hard to get
And hope she lets me win.

I think I'll stay home
And bother my baby.
I think I'll stay home
And get in her hair.
I think I'll stay home
And bother my baby.
And maybe if I stay home
I'll get somewhere.[2]

The best part of being together as friends is the way that our time with each other can become the golden thread of memories that are often sewn into the fabric of marriage. That bright cord may very well become the most beautiful and visible part of a lifetime together in times of reminiscing.

Steve: An example of one of the strands in our golden thread of memories centers around a deck we had built onto the back of our house. It was added so we could park our car there and enter with groceries and other bags. It would save us from having to walk all the way around to the front.

We hired a carpenter to build the deck and also to turn a second-story window into a door. After he completed the deck portion, we (I) made the dumb mistake of going ahead and paying for both jobs in full. Unfortunately, the carpenter skipped out and left us with an unfinished job. Unable to contact him, and totally frustrated, we (I) finally decided that we'd just do it ourselves.

First, I rented a masonry saw to cut the brick veneer. (If you've never seen a brick saw, it looks sort of like a Volkswagen Bug with a blade. It's huge!) After making the cut, I then removed the inside drywall and window frame. I had no idea what I was doing, but I was determined to "make a memory," which, Annie says, is sometimes another term for destructive behavior.

Several hours later, with a gaping hole in our backside wall, I stood proudly on the new deck and looked into the house at Annie standing in the kitchen. Through a throat full of brick and drywall dust, I said to her, "Now what?" Really, I didn't have a clue what to do next.

Annie kindly suggested that we call a friend who was good at carpentry and ask him what to do. He came over, walked up on our freshly built deck, and looked with amazement at the huge hole in the house. With a polite stutter in his voice, as if he was afraid to ask, he pointed to the ugly opening and said, "Did you do this?"

With a Jimmy Carter-sized grin on my face I answered with a proud, "Yes, sir!"

Our friend's face turned from a quizzical look to a friendly frown as he said, "Do you realize that people's houses fall in from doing stuff like that!"

We groveled, and then we (I) begged him for his help. He agreed to come back that evening, and as he left he told us what to buy at the lumber store to complete the job. That night, around 10, with his assistance, we had a door where a window used to be. We were elated...and relieved that the house was still standing.

It was not too long after that dangerous and exciting episode that the following song was written to commemorate these kinds of mutual accomplishments. The lyric also recognizes that our memories, like the one I just shared, are special mostly to the two that make them. Thus, the reason for their value.

When Memories Turn to Gold

We made another memory today,
We thought it was beautiful.
Someone else may look and say,
"Why, it's nothing so unusual."
But someday they will turn to gold,
These memories we gather.
And there's a reason we must hold
Tightly to these treasures.

'Cause we're holding on to something
That only two can share.
And when only two can touch them
It makes them rich and rare.
And someday when we sit and spin
These yarns within our souls,
For you and me
That will be
When our memories turn to gold.

So one by one we'll gather them
Memories for our winter
They'll warm our hearts someday when
Our days are cold and bitter.[3]

R—Respect One Another with Your Words

"There is one who speaks rashly like the thrusts of a sword, but the tongue of the wise brings healing." This verse from Proverbs 12:18 is sobering as it is, but when a closer look is taken at the passage, it is even more poignant. The two words *sword* and *tongue* indicate a very up-close-and-personal aspect of communication. While an arrow can be launched in battle and fly long distances to a random, unknown target, the tongue is short like a dagger and is a face-to-face weapon. It knows its victim very well.

Though the tongue can often kill a friendship, it can also revive it. Keep in mind the truth from Proverbs 18:21 that says, "Death and life are in the power of the tongue."

In our desire to help you choose the "life" side of that verse, we offer four types of words that can keep the love flowing through your friendship.

1. *Appropriate Words*—**"Like apples of gold in settings of silver is a word spoken in right circumstances" (Proverbs 25:11).**

Steve: A good example of a moment when I heard Annie say an appropriate word (actually there were 17 of them) happened the day we brought home our brand-new vehicle. We parked it in the driveway and admired it for a minute or two and then went about our chores at home. I decided it would be a good day to put a weather sealant on our wood deck. I proceeded to the garage and gathered up the spray pump and can of sealant.

As I sprayed a fine mist of the chemical onto the deck, I was not aware that a gentle breeze was blowing toward the new car, carrying with it tiny droplets of the contents of the pressurized container. After completing the task I walked by the car on the way to the garage and noticed that the silver finish on the hood had a pimpled look. That's when it suddenly dawned on me what had happened. Our brand-new ride looked like it had a bad case of acne. I was devastated. But more than that I dreaded to tell Annie what a dumb mistake I had made.

I'll never forget the stunned look on her face when I broke the news. Her jaw dropped, and she just stared at me. Feeling totally deserving of a good tongue-thrashing, I waited for her comments. That's when I learned a huge lesson about appropriate words. Her expression slowly changed to pity and she said, "I know you didn't mean to do such a thing. Is there any way to fix it?"

Wow! I felt like a huge weight was lifted off my back. By showing me instant mercy, my mind was free to search for a way to heal the ugly scars that the chemical had caused on our new hood. Within about two hours, I had carefully popped all the paint bubbles. With a matching color of touch-up paint, our new vehicle was back to very near normal. Annie later quipped, "We should be proud. We have the most unique car on the block!" It was another appropriate word.

Annie's kindness in the face of my Ford folly inspired me to show some mercy and grace with my words when two checks that held her signature did the rubber ball act. One good word deserves another!

2. *Reproving Words*—Proverbs 25:12 NKJV: "Like an earring of gold and an ornament of fine gold is a wise rebuker to an obedient ear." Proverbs 17:10: "A rebuke goes deeper into one who has understanding than a hundred blows into a fool."

Annie: While appropriate words in times of blunder and failure are welcome, there are occasions when a word of rebuke is equally fitting. For instance, many years ago, prior to our dating days, something happened that required quite a risk on my part. Yet, the outcome was positive.

Steve had invited me to come to his parents' home and listen to a song he had recorded on his reel-to-reel tape deck. As we stood in the basement on that summer day in 1973, I listened closely to his 11 verse, very Bob Dylanesque type song. It took around five minutes to play. When it was over, Steve stopped the tape and asked me a question I dreaded. "What do you think?"

I debated quickly with myself about whether or not to offer an honest opinion. I opted for truth and said, "It sounds like the product of a very confused mind."

Poor Steve. As if I had just gored his pet dog, he bowed his head and didn't say a word. Then, he looked up and humbly said something in hippie dialect I'll never forget. "Cool! You're absolutely right, and you've given a very thoughtful observation. Thank you for listening so closely. Far out."

That day I saw something very attractive about Steve. Although he might have received a very honest opinion, his humility in how he took it made me think that he would be someone worth getting to know.

3. *Refreshing Words*—"Like the cold of snow in the time of harvest is a faithful messenger to those who send him, for he refreshes the soul of his masters" (Proverbs 25:13).

Like blowing on the back of a sweaty baby or fanning an overheated companion, refreshing words revive and comfort. Here are some examples:

- I'm pregnant
- I'm not pregnant
- My mother can't come visit for the month
- The kids are going to be gone all day
- You look pretty
- You don't have to cook tonight
- I found your keys
- I found your wallet
- It was on sale
- I fixed the mower

• I think the goldfish is dead

• I'm ready to mulch

Words like these, in the heat of the everydayness of life, can refresh like a glass of lemonade carried to your spouse who's working in the yard on a sultry summer day.

4. Kind Words—"Pleasant words are a honeycomb, sweet to the soul and healing to the bones" (Proverbs 16:24).

Annie: There is one thing I like about the time that Steve spends in the woods. He says he sees a lot out there that reminds him of me. One day he came home with a song lyric that he had written while on the deer stand. This song is my favorite example of kind words.

Love Song of the Hunter

When I see the sunrise I think of you
How you're faithful and true to me
When I hear the bluebird's morning refrain
I hear your name so lovely.

Sunny skies, your eyes
Sweet smell of the pine
Brings you to my mind.
And when I walk these fields
Where the bonnets are blue
It's a lovely view
And I think of you.

When I see the ivy that grows on the vine
I think of the time you grew on me.
And when I see the young fawns in the meadow at play
I think of the way I am with you.

Sunny skies, your eyes
A warm April wind
Your touch on my skin.
And when I walk these fields
Where the bonnets are blue
It's a lovely view
And I think of you.

Sunny skies
Your eyes
The dance of the stars
Your love in my heart
And when I walk these fields
Where the bonnets are blue
It's a lovely view
And I think of you[4]

I—Include Your Spouse's Ideas in the Plan

Annie: Anyone who has ever tried to rekindle a friendship knows it takes time and effort. In the past few pages we have shown that being a friend includes such things as doing fun activities together and using words to soothe and comfort. Another key ingredient in keeping a friendship alive is to *value the other's opinion.*

One wife said, "I never have any input into where we go on vacation. My husband thinks because he works every day that we should go wherever he wants. It's all about him. After all these years, I don't even bother to give my opinion. I know it won't do any good."

True friends defer to one another. For instance, if we have a Saturday free, Steve and I take turns choosing where we want to spend our afternoon. Sometimes we may go to an antique mall and just walk around, or we might go to an antique auto show and look at the cars. (I'll let you guess who chooses which!) However, no one person should make all the plans. Philippians 2:3-4, as we mentioned earlier, holds the key to valuing one another: "Do nothing from selfishness or empty conceit, but with humility of mind regard one another as more important than yourselves; do not merely look out for your own personal interests, but also for the interests of others."

We have found that as we strive to live by this principle of putting the other's need and interest above our own, God gives us the power to overcome our bent toward selfishness, which, as we all know, is a killer of friendship.

E—Enjoy Life by Rediscovering Laughter

Annie: Steve came in from hunting one day and asked, "Annie, how do you keep a turkey in suspense?"

I didn't have a clue. However, after about eight seconds of silence, and watching a silly smirk grow on my husband's face, I got the joke. (If you're still trying to answer his question, he got you, too!)

If there's one thing I've learned from my sweetheart, it would be that Proverbs 17:22 is true: "A joyful heart is good medicine, but a broken spirit dries up the bones."

The seriousness of life can literally suck the air out of us. A permanent scowl, if we're not careful, can replace the laughter and smiles of a more carefree time in our lives. One wife and mother was lamenting her cheerless existence. "I remember a time when people thought I was funny. I had friends who wanted to be with me. Now, life is so hard and, somehow, it has changed me. Even I can't stand to be around me."

There's one sad truth to keep in mind. Life is probably not going to get much easier. Therefore, if our lives are to improve, we're the ones who are going to have to make the difference. As husbands and wives, we can consciously help restore joy and laughter in our marriages.

One idea for a fun evening might be to rent or buy a comedy movie and watch it together. We especially enjoy the old Jerry Lewis flicks because they are free of unacceptable language and lack the "skin" that is often the cheap feature of later titles. If you're like us, you've tried renting the newer films, only to be disappointed. A movie might be humorous, but it might also be offensive. But there's good news. A recent remedy to the dilemma of questionable movies is found inside our VCR. Some brands offer what is called the "TV Guardian." Using the closed caption signal on tapes and DVDs, this amazing technology screens and mutes any bad language or any use of the Lord's name that is inappropriate. A couple must still be vigilante in choosing good, wholesome entertainment, but this device can help alleviate one obstacle.

One other idea: Be on the lookout for something funny to share with your spouse at the end of the day. Having an attitude of humor can change any dreary day into a party. Viennese psychiatrist Dr. Victor Frankl was imprisoned in a Nazi concentration camp during World War II. Needless to say, finding amusement in that setting was not an easy task. However, his desire to see his wife again motivated him to find a way to survive the horrors of his existence. He and another prisoner determined that every day they would think of one funny thing that could happen to them after they were released. Each day they would share their ideas with each other and laugh. He said, "Humor was another of the soul's weapons in the fight for self-preservation. It is well known that humor, more than anything else in the human makeup, can afford an aloofness and an ability to rise above any situation, even if only for a few seconds."[5]

N—Notice the Small Things a Spouse Does

I don't know anyone who doesn't want to be recognized and appreciated for what he or she does. When we asked husbands and wives to share what made them feel happy in their marriages, often the answers revolved around simple, little things that their spouses noticed and then expressed verbal appreciation for it.

Here are some responses to the question, "I love it when my husband says…":

- Dinner was wonderful. No one can cook like you!

- You do an incredible job with the children.

- I appreciate the way you keep the house so clean.

- Thank you for exercising and keeping your body so fit.

Husbands responded to the sentence, "I love it when my wife says…":

- Thank you for fixing things around the house. I'm so blessed to have a man like you. You can fix anything!

- I love it when you fill the car up with gas. I know I should have taken care of it, but I'm glad you did it.

- I appreciate you paying the bills and keeping our records so organized.

- You do a great job as a dad. The children adore you!

As is evident by these comments, it is obvious that nothing feels so good as to hear the words "thank you" and "I appreciate all you've done." These verbal kudos and the attentive attitude go a long way in solidifying a lifelong marital friendship.

D—Dole Out the Cash

If the best things in life are free, why would an element of friendship include the spending of money? True enough, some of the most fun we've had as friends and lovers have required the expenditure of little or no cash. The walks down our country roads with the smell of tobacco barns bellowing out their sweet, aromatic scent (you have to have been raised on a farm to fully appreciate the nostalgic appeal of such an experience) have yielded priceless evenings of enjoyment for us.

While it is true that we don't always have to spend the dough to make the bread of memories, money can be an excellent ingredient in a friendship. Buying little things for each other is usually a good way to display our appreciation for the other. Or, in some cases, another way to show a spouse that we like them is to offer them the freedom to spend some dollars on themselves.

The key to a couple successfully handling this "hot potato" in the area of cash outgo is, very simply, to be fair. Without both husband and wife having equal access to the fun-money fund, the potential for hurt feelings is too great.

Steve: I understand the need to be fair with money. But I didn't always get this point. I was awakened to it one hunting season when I came home with another dozen aluminum arrows. At the time, they cost about $3.50 each without the broadheads (another $4 to $6 each). Annie had seen my big bucket that was already full of arrows from previous seasons. When she saw the bundle of 12 more, she nicely asked, "Did you need those?"

I answered, "Oh! Yes, ma'am. I need new sticks every year!"

A month or so later we were at one of those restaurants that has a craft store in the front. We finished eating, and I went to the counter to pay for the meal. After I got my receipt, I turned around and saw Annie taking Christmas ornaments off a rack. One by one she removed the dainty works of seasonal art. As she did, I walked up and with an unhappy tone in my voice I asked, "What are you doing?" Translated, my question was, "Do you need those?"

Annie never broke stride with her hands as she took another ornament off the shelf. Then, without looking at me, she said, "I'm buying arrows."

I headed to the truck in silence—like any smart man would do!

When it comes to being fair with money, the way I like to put it to the husbands is, *We have to buck up and doe the right thing!* And, I offer this wise tip: If you go out and buy something that enhances your hobby— whatever its cost might be—give your wife its equal value in cash. (Of course, this idea doesn't apply to purchases like Ranger Bass Boats. That hefty an item definitely requires your mutual agreement!) The fact is, and I know from experience, this "equal value in cash" idea will accomplish two very important things. One, it will curb your spending. And two, it'll win you points with your honey. And, remember, as I said earlier, if you're a deer hunter...points *are* important!

S—*Sympathize with One Another*—"Rejoice with those who rejoice, and weep with those who weep. Be of the same mind toward one another" (Romans 12:15).

Annie: I once heard it said that a spouse is someone who can double the joys and halve the sorrows. Thankfully, that's the kind of friend I've found in my husband, Steve. For instance, the caring sympathy he showed me when I lost my mother to cancer, and then two years later when my dad died will be something I will cherish until *I* die. Prior to suffering such great losses, I never realized just how important it was to have my mate also be my caring friend.

I was additionally anguished when, not long after my mother passed away, I witnessed a sorrowful contrast. A close friend's mother also died, and I went to the wake to pay my respects. I was surprised and saddened to find my friend standing all alone at the casket. I learned that her husband had decided not to come to the funeral home for the visitation because he said, "It makes me feel awkward to be around all those grieving people." My honest reaction? I wanted to find him and slap his jaws! How could he have done that to her? If ever she needed him to set aside his own needs and sense of comfort, it was at a time such as that. However, she didn't seem surprised by his insensitivity. After all, she lived with it every day.

Now, just for the sake of conversation, let's give this guy the benefit of the doubt. Perhaps he was indeed reluctant to come with her to the funeral home because he didn't know what to say or do in that situation. While that may have been the case, I have found that during stressful, grief-filled times, the hurting spouse is more likely to receive words of comfort if they are supported by an attitude of sympathy. Like someone once said, "No one cares how much you know, until they know how much you care."

H—Help One Another

We were amazed at the number of women who responded to our questionnaire inquiry that asked, "How do you and your husband relate in the area of household chores?" Their answers revealed different levels of cooperation in the domestic department. Here are a few of the ladies' answers:

- He procrastinates and is a slow worker.

- He does his work, and I do mine.

- He forgets to put on his glasses or turn the lights on, which means he misses dirty spots on the dishes.

- He does household repairs but is not too helpful with the day-to-day chores. I work outside the home, and it is all left to me.

- He does nothing around the house, but he wants me and the kids to fix everything.

- He hesitates to fix things because he doesn't feel capable.

- He is very cooperative and does a lot of things.

- He washes the dishes three days a week.

- He doesn't appreciate what I do, and it's frustrating when I ask him to repair something and he doesn't.

- He says he doesn't care if the house is messy. We have two small kids, and it's hard for me to get anything done.

- He is awesome! He helps me so much I feel guilty.

- I don't think he was raised to do "women's work," which means he doesn't help me at home at all.

- He possesses the ability to do anything, but he's too busy to do anything.

- He's great at fixing things or at finding the right person to do it if he can't.

- He thinks I'm nagging if I ask him to do anything.

- The only thing he cares about being in good working order is the TV.

- He never complains about anything I ask him to do.

When we asked the men to respond to this same question about their wives, the number-one answer, without listing all of their comments, was, "I wish she would learn how to operate some of our small equipment and learn to do some small repairs." A few of their ideas included mowing, changing furnace air filters and light bulbs, splicing electric extension cords, and hanging pictures and curtain rods.

Some of these men expressed their concern that if they suddenly became a product of the statistic that most husbands precede their wives in death, their wives might be helpless in too many areas of house care. Many of the men said they were willing to teach their wives how to do some of the jobs but found resistance. Her help seemed very important to these men—not to get out of a job, but to prepare for the future.

In a nutshell, the one question that a spouse would bless the other with in terms of being a helper around the house is, "What can I do today to make your life less stressful?" And when the answer is given, go do it!

I—*Isolate Yourselves*

A good gauge for whether or not two people are true friends is if they enjoy being alone together from time to time—just the two of them away from the crowds. This observation doesn't necessarily include young couples like our former neighbors who are parents to four small children. They were sometimes starved for conversation with other adults, and often they would tuck their energetic kids into bed and then call us. We would go over and have coffee and give them some grown-up company. They needed our "maturity." However, the couples we are concerned about have a different attitude.

We've observed husbands and wives who come to our marriage events who, when we give them free time to spend together, head off with a big group. They spend their free time with the men talking to men and women to women. While it may be true that some may use the time to fellowship and catch up with friends, we fear that some choose the crowd as a way of avoiding each other. We wonder at times if they have lost the desire and the skill to have meaningful and timely conversation with their spouses. If this describes your relationship, perhaps these conversation starters will help the next time the two of you are alone. But first, three rules: take turns answering each question, listen and don't talk while the other is answering, and no negative comments allowed.

1. Tell me about your best friend when you were a kid.

2. What is your favorite childhood memory?

3. What is the funniest thing that has happened to you in the past five years?

4. Where is one place you've always wanted to go? Can we make a five-year plan to go there together?

5. Is there a hobby we could do together?

P—Publicly Proclaim Appreciation

Annie: We previously noted that a good friend/mate will notice the little things that a spouse does and thank him or her. This is done mostly in private, and it is a very good thing to do. But occasionally, it is a blessing for the other to "overhear" words of praise for them that is offered to others. It would bring a delight to a spouse—the kind of joy that Jesus might have felt when His Father in heaven said *about* Him to the doubters that stood nearby: "This is my beloved Son, in whom I am well-pleased" (Matthew 3:17). It was a statement said indirectly to Christ, but it must have gone directly to the heart of our Lord. This kind of public proclamation of praise for spouses brings pleasure to their souls.

With that in mind, I make this public statement. Long before Steve and I married, I found this old poem. All these years later, I have seen how the words are true about him. I still feel this way about him…

Tribute to Friendship

I love you not only for what you are,
But for what I am when I am with you;
I love you not only for what you have made of yourself,
But for what you are making of me;

I love you not for closing your ears to the discords in me,
But for adding to the music in me by worshipful listening;
You have done it without a touch, without a word, without a sign.
You have done it just by being yourself.
Perhaps that is what being a friend means, after all.[6]

May God bless your friendship.

seven

Making a Living
or Making a Killing

*A*nnie: It was a cold March day. It had been raining earlier in the morning, but by two o'clock in the afternoon the weather had given a temporary reprieve. The intermittent hints of sunshine brightened everyone's spirits.

The nervous young bride stood in the back of the church, making one last, soul-searching decision as to whether to take the arm of her father, who was patiently standing beside her, and plunge into the unknown life of matrimony. As she glanced down the short aisle of the Methodist church, she saw her groom waiting with the preacher. The young man was attired in a homemade shirt that was cut from a bolt of unbleached muslin cotton, lime green polyester pants, and a pair of brown, well-worn leather boots. Much to the mother-in-law's bewilderment, there was no tuxedo with ruffled shirt and gold-plated cuff-links. There was definitely no tie or shiny, patent leather shoes. His "outside the line" outfit was the preferred fashion statement of the mid-1970s hippie…simple and cheap.

He was not the only one influenced by the era. The bride was standing next to her well-dressed father in her homespun wedding dress that boasted a total cost of $30. On her feet were the comfortable $2 shoes she had thankfully found on the rack at the local five-and-dime. With a crown of fresh cut flowers gracing her long brown, parted-in-the-middle hair, she finally, and bravely, gave the nod to the pianist.

When she slowly began to walk down the aisle to the unusual wedding music selection of "All Hail the Power of Jesus' Name," the witnesses that filled the pews immediately realized that a very nontraditional wedding had begun. After about 45 minutes of scripture reading and other rambling admonitions, the vows were exchanged and the ceremony was complete. The 100 guests were then invited to the basement fellowship hall for a simple reception of cake and punch. The day ended with two young people happily climbing into a borrowed car and driving off to their future together.

The ceremony I just described was Steve's and my wedding. A beautiful and priceless memory we will cherish for all times. (Actually, "priceless" is the right word because the total cost of the event was a mere $200!)You may be wondering why it was such a humble affair and could more have been spent on such an important day in our lives? The answer, of course, is yes. I suppose we could have done what many penniless young couples do. We could have let our parents go into debt, spend funds they didn't have, and "charged" themselves into our matrimonial bliss. But because we strongly embraced the "stay simple and stay free" mind-set of the times, we held to a different attitude about money, and we were not about to let debt happen on our account.

While there is much that could have been better about the "hippie era," one good thing about it was the attitude of simple living that had influenced us. Money seemed to have been important only if it helped a person maintain a lifestyle of sharing. At the time, at least in our circles of friends, it wasn't "cool" to be so encumbered with stuff. In fact, as we prepared to marry, Steve suggested, for example, that I reduce my inventory of shoes from two pairs to one. He did so in hopes that if we had to move quickly, our limited number of "things" could be packed in a matter of hours instead of days. I realize that admission sounds like we were criminals on the run from the law, but that is not the case. We were not running *from* something…we were running *to* something, that is, a life of peace…man! Whether it was a product of rebellion against the "establishment" or just trying to fit in, the attitude of simplicity was a jewel that was mined from the cave of confusion that young people lived in during those years. But sadly, that era seems to have passed. A very different mentality marks our current time. (And oddly enough, many of those who once embraced the uncluttered lifestyle of the hippie days are the very ones entrenched in the glut of possessions today.)

I recently got a glimpse of the difference between the way we thought about money in the mid-1970s and now when I heard the words of a young groom-to-be. He was living with his girlfriend outside of the bonds of marriage and was asked by his worried mother, "When are the two of you going to get married?"

With a tone of voice that let his behind-the-times mom know that he thought her question was utterly ridiculous, he replied, "We can't afford to get married until I can buy her a diamond ring. It needs to be at least two carats in size."

I couldn't believe my ears. Somewhere along the way, between our long-gone era and now, the attitude pendulum has taken a wide swing in terms of how young people think about money. And, it seems, the "ring is everything" attitude is one of the clearest commentaries of this swing.

While it is frustrating to think that such an intense emphasis is too often placed on the monetary and mass value of the ring, we were not exempt from facing that particular sign of our times. We personally went through the "ring thing" when our daughter, Heidi, was engaged. (We tell this with permission and a promise to say that the following description of how Heidi dealt with the diamond dilemma does not at all represent who she is now.)

Although she and her future husband, Emmitt, had already decided to get married, he was still in the process of picking out and paying for an engagement ring. He was a senior in college, working a part-time job for the school and paying for his tuition. The money he needed for the token of his intentions was steadily being saved, but was taking longer than Heidi had anticipated. Actually, she fought a feeling of embarrassment over her "naked" finger. Even though she knew it was just a matter of time, she began to show impatience.

Since I didn't receive an engagement ring myself (remember, we were poor hippies!), I was not at all sympathetic to Heidi's plight. I kept reminding her that Emmitt had given her his promise, and that his word was more binding and more important than any piece of jewelry. I reminded her, "You can lose a ring, but you have to break a promise."

What I was not taking into account was the tremendous amount of peer pressure Heidi was under at college. When a couple announced to everyone at school that they were going to get married, the first thing the bride-to-be's friends would say is, "Show us your ring!"

I began to understand Heidi's predicament when she relayed a conversation she had with a friend from college. The young lady said, "If my fiancé doesn't pick out a big enough ring, I'm going to make him take it back and get me a better one." Oh, I pity that young man! Another young suitor was looking at rings with his girlfriend. She kept asking to see the largest stones and the most expensive settings. When she settled on a $10,000 diamond, the boy said, "I can't afford that kind of ring." Her reply said it all, "That's all right, you can put it on your credit card and make payments." He dumped her the next day, and rightly so. He had a preview of what his life was going to be like for the next 50 years. He was smart, like the young fellow in this story...

Not the Ring

The Dollar Store took over
The Murphy five-and-dime
But Bobby's wage was not affected
By the changing of the times

So he gave up his old Malibu
He got three fifty dollar bills
Then he walked downtown to buy the ring
That would show the love he feels

The change was seven dollars
And he headed to her door
And rehearsed the words he'd say
When his knee was on the floor

But some girls have expectations
Diamonds in their eyes
Sometimes they measure love
By the rule of cost and size
They can't see that...

Diamonds can be stolen
Silver can be broken
The treasure that's worth more than anything
Is in the promise, not the ring.

When she looked into the little white paper box
That was shaking in his hand

She laughed as if she'd heard a joke
She didn't understand

Well now Bobby drives that Malibu
Took four fifty dollar bills
And there's a girl who'll never know the wealth
In the love that Bobby feels

Diamonds can be stolen
Silver can be broken
The treasure that's worth more than anything
Is in the promise, not the ring.[1]

Much to Heidi's credit, she began to realize that her impatience with the "ring delay" was not only childish, but she regretted putting the emphasis on the wrong thing. She soon resolved that it's not the ring that keeps a couple together, nor are they held together by the elaborate wedding ceremony with the hordes of attendants and flowers that make the matrimonial ritual special and effective. (And furthermore, the wedding day is not the only important day of your life. Instead, it's every day afterward that matters.) It's the committed promise to live, love, and serve one another that is the diamond of greatest value.

As for me not having a ring, here's the update. When we got married in 1975, I used a borrowed wedding band for a few weeks. Then during that summer while we were walking through the vendor aisles at the Tennessee State Fair, we came across some wedding rings that were being sold for $2 each. We made the big purchase. However, there was a problem.

One day while at the dentist's office, the doctor looked at my hand and saw that the skin around the little ring on my finger had turned green. Feeling pity for us he asked if he could take our bands for a few days. We turned them over to him, unaware of what he had in mind. He called us about a week later and asked us to come to his office. Using dental gold, our kindhearted dentist had covered the little bands, making them truly a treasure. We wore them for a few years then replaced that set with a slight upgrade found at a Service Merchandise store. Then on our twenty-fifth anniversary, Steve gave me a long-awaited gift. It was an incredibly beautiful set of diamond rings. He had waited a quarter of a century to make that financial step.

Times Have Changed (and Change Is All We Have Left)

No doubt, the difference in attitude toward "stuff" has shifted through the years. However, the change between our parents' economic attitude of the 40s and 50s and that of our own is not quite as distinct as the difference between ours of the 60s and 70s and the new millennium. Essentially, it seems that in the 1940s and 1950s the goal was to *make a living*. When our parents were first getting started in their post-World War II era, there was a certain sense of satisfaction with simply providing stability for the family. Their first purchase of a dwelling was not just a house. Nor was it purchased for the purpose of making a "status" point. Instead, for them, the house would become their lifetime homeplace where they assumed they'd raise their kids and even die there.

As the years progressed, however, things have drastically changed. When young couples look at a house on the market today, very often they don't view it as a place where they might live till the end. Instead, many of them refer to a first house as a "starter home." In other words, they think, "This house will have to do until we can do better."

The starter home approach is perhaps some of the best evidence that a financially dangerous mind-set exists in young couples in this era. While the goal for newlyweds used to be to make a living, today it's…*let's make a killing*.

Sadly, as most of us know, the pursuit of money and the "upgrades" it can buy have placed a tremendous amount of pressure on the relationships between husbands and wives. Buying on credit, for example, is one of the most commonly accepted means by which we are able to easily acquire the "stuff" that can supposedly enhance our lives and make us appear successful. However, that kind of money has a terrible price tag. This unwanted cost is evidenced by the following comments from husbands and wives in response to our questionnaire. We asked them, "What is your greatest concern regarding the financial health of your family?"

Wives

- I feel paralyzed and helpless because I don't see a way out of debt.

- Almost all of our debt is due to the misuse of credit cards.

- My husband likes to buy tools and cars on credit, and we can't afford either.

- I fear God will punish us for getting into such a financial mess.

- After declaring bankruptcy, we committed to control our credit card spending, but it has been very difficult to follow through and not get back into trouble.

- I use credit cards to buy things I really don't need, but I use them to fill a void because my husband is never home.

- Retiring seems out of the realm of possibility for us because of our credit card debt.

- I fear we may lose our home due to debt.

- Our younger years of spending (before kids) messed up our credit, and now we're paying for it.

Husbands

- All of our income is required to pay for credit cards.

- We're stuck in a five-year van lease that we can't afford, but we can't find a way out of it. The stress this causes on our finances has hurt our marriage because I get the blame.

- We overestimated our ability to buy a home. The mortgage is eating us alive.

- The sign that the sibling rivalry demon reared its ugly head is sitting in our garage. The note we have to cover on our "ride" has caused some serious tension between the two of us.

- We made a huge mistake by charging our ten-day vacation to credit cards. The whole time we were out we fought about how much to spend. I hate to admit it but the vacation was only an addition to the balance. I know I need to take charge and do some plastic surgery, but it's hard to do it. We argue a lot over this issue.

It is obvious by the comments offered by these troubled husbands and wives that money—the use and abuse of it—affects the marriage relationship. One well-respected financial advisor said that over 56 percent of married couples, at some time, cite money issues as more important than sex in their marriage. That fact can be borne out as we look at some additional comments made by the husbands and wives who were willing to share their concerns about how their financial situation influenced their relationships.

As you will see, a few of the observations that are made concerning the fiscal health of the family are quite positive; however, sadly enough, most indicate hearts that are frightened and frustrated.

Wives

- Our financial situation is like a dark cloud over my head.

- I stay home with the children and don't feel that I contribute to our needs.

- We use our credit cards, but we pay them off every month. We owe no one.

- My medical problems have put a heavy strain on our finances, and I feel guilty.

- We fight over who spends more.

- We really need to be on a budget.

- If I can't pay cash, I don't buy it, even though it's hard to do sometimes.

- Needs of in-laws keeps me from working.

- I panic when we have to dip into our savings.

- A tornado took our farm, and now we deal with depression and anger.

- My husband is very liberal with spending, and it worries me.

- My husband's lack of employment is depleting our life's savings.

- I don't trust the stock market, and my husband wants to invest heavily.

- Tithing has always been a priority for my husband and me, and God has blessed us for it.

- My husband and I fight over money, or the lack of it, due to his gambling problem.

- Sometimes I lie about my spending.

- We argue if I spend too much on our grandchildren.

Husbands

- My wife wants to know why I spend so much time working—it's because she spends her time spending the money I earn.

- My wife wants to buy things without saving for it.

- I feel really bad because we don't tithe our money.

- My wife doesn't want to be on a budget.

- I'm worried about retirement.

- We don't save enough.

- My wife tells me I'm not good at managing our money.

- My wife spends too much on others when we don't have enough for ourselves.

- My wife doesn't want me to see the bills because of her over-spending.

- I often hear the complaint that I'm not involved enough in our finances.

- She says we don't set aside enough for emergency expenses.

- I worry that we don't spend enough on our loved ones.

- My wife and I lack compatibility in the area of spending. I'm the spender and she's the saver.

- I can't seem to satisfy my wife's desire for money.

- I want to tithe, but my wife doesn't think we can afford it.

- My wife complains that I work too much, but if I don't we will not make ends meet.

- She worries about the bills, and I try to encourage her not to fret because things always seem to work out.

- I wish my wife would learn more about handling money. I worry about what she would do if I die.

- My wife and I do not talk much about money.

- My wife works, and I do not at this time. I feel terribly unac-complished.

What can we conclude that husbands and wives aren't telling each other about money?

> "We need to make a change in our fiscal focus. The pres-sure to achieve financial success and to accumulate and pay for all our possessions is hurting our marriage. I don't want to fight about money anymore. I want to make it our goal, as a couple, to be satisfied with making a living, instead of trying to make a killing."

How does a couple "go back" once they've entered the rat race of materialism? Is the dilemma, as some of the husbands and wives indi-cated in the answers, that they simply don't make enough money? Is it a numbers problem? Or is the impasse found in the fact that they haven't landed on a budget they can both agree on...and stay on?

These important questions require the wisdom of the money experts. There are many excellent organizations and ministries designed to help couples learn to budget their funds. Some even offer help in finding more lucrative employment, which may help alleviate a financial crunch. We will leave the giving of specific financial advice to the professionals. Instead of addressing the "how to" in the money han-dling department of marriage, it is more important to consider why money is often the hungry little fox that spoils the entire vineyard (see Song of Solomon 2:15).

God and Money

The Bible has much to say about money. Dr. John MacArthur, in his commentary on the book of Matthew, says it well:

> Whether men are wealthy or poor—or somewhere in between—their attitude toward material possessions is one of the most reliable marks of their spiritual condi-tion....There is a temptation to both the rich and the

poor. The rich are tempted to trust their possessions, and the poor are tempted to doubt God's provision. The rich are tempted to become self-satisfied in the false security of their riches, and the poor are tempted to worry and fear in the insecurity of their poverty....One of the supreme tests of our spiritual lives is gauged by how we view and handle money. Sixteen of the thirty-eight parables of Jesus deal with money. One out of every ten verses in the New Testament deals with the subject. Scripture offers about five hundred verses on prayer, fewer than five hundred on faith, and over two thousand on money.[2]

We can conclude from the frequency of the biblical mention of money that God is extremely interested in how we think about and handle resources. With as much attention as He gave to the issue, how grievous it must be to Him when passages about money are misunderstood and misused. For example, consider this familiar, often misquoted reference to 1 Timothy 6:10: "It's just like the Bible says, money is the root of all evil."

Although the mistake is slight, the impact is severe. It's not the "money" that is evil, it's the *love* of it that gets us into trouble. The verses surrounding this familiar passage give us the true warning of exactly what the "little hungry fox" is that eats away at the one specific thing that can keep us out of a lot of fiscal trouble.

But godliness actually is a means of great gain when accompanied by *contentment*. For we have brought nothing into the world, so we cannot take anything out of it either. If we have food and covering, with these we shall be content [making a living!]. But those who want to get rich [making a killing!] fall into temptation and a snare and many foolish and harmful desires which plunge men into ruin and destruction. *For the love of money is a root of all sorts of evil*, and some by longing for it have wandered away from the faith and pierced themselves with many griefs....Instruct those who are rich in this present world not to be conceited or to fix their hope on the uncertainty of riches, but on God, who richly supplies us with all things to enjoy" (1 Timothy 6:6-10,17, emphasis added).

Content but Not Lazy

What is contentment? We propose that it is "wanting what you have rather than having what you want." By encouraging you to have a renewed appreciation for the financial state you may be in at this moment, in no way are we suggesting that a husband or wife just sit down, forget ambition, and never work another day. One fellow said, "Money doesn't grow on trees. You have to beat the bushes for it!" Proverbs 6:10 offers just one of the Bible's many warnings about laziness: "A little sleep, a little slumber, a little folding of the hands to rest—your poverty will come in like a vagabond and your need like an armed man."

Annie: Taking the scripture seriously in regard to avoiding laziness can result in some seriously sore muscles. For example, every house we've ever lived in, I've loved. Despite any shortcomings the structure might have had, I've always had as my goal to make it the best home possible for my family. It was a happy day for me when I realized that being content doesn't mean sitting back and making no changes.

The first house we bought (yes, our "starter home") was a sweet little house in a well-established neighborhood. It had been a rental house before we rescued it, and there was a lot of work that needed to be done on it. The purchase price was $28,500.

One of the many projects I personally took on was removing some nasty, old carpet from the basement steps. (I waited until Steve went out of town. I knew he would think I was insane—which I was—for tackling such a task.) After I eliminated the filthy floor covering I discovered the steps were constructed of nothing more than rough lumber. Since sandpaper was cheaper than renting an electric sander I began the endless, backbreaking job of manually smoothing each step down to a planed, shiny gloss. Ignoring the fact that my entire body had never ached so badly, at the end of a long day, I brushed on the polyurethane sealer and went to bed.

A couple of hours later I was awakened by horrendous muscle spasms throughout my arms, neck, and back. The convulsive movement curled my toes and shook the bed. Realizing there would be little sleep that night, I got up and turned on the hottest water I could stand and filled the bathtub full. I spent most of the night soaking in a scalding reservoir of water trying to relieve the throbbing pain.

Despite the agony of aching muscles, no one could have been more proud of those stairs. The accumulative effect of all of the similar small improvements we made over the years proved financially beneficial. After 11 years of living in that house, we sold it for $71,000. Using the profits from that sale of the first house, along with some savings we sacrificially socked away, we were able to buy a house closer to the school where our children were attending at the time. Gratefully, the house we acquired was purchased with cash. Again, with contentment as our goal, we were able to move into a house and leave the mortgage payment behind. There's no question we could have procured a nicer place if we had secured a mortgage loan. However, by being willing to accept an adequate house, rather than the best we could afford, we gained something of much greater value. We won freedom from the slavery of debt.

Looking successful and having all of the trappings that great wealth brings is not as much fun as one might anticipate. Andrew Carnegie, the American industrialist and philanthropist who founded the iron and steel industry in the United States, was quoted as saying, "Millionaires who laugh are rare. My experience is that wealth is apt to take the smiles away." Isn't that interesting? Those of us who look from the outside in on those with unimaginable wealth might be surprised at the lack of happiness that sometimes accompanies such great possessions. John D. Rockefeller Jr., one on the wealthiest men in the world, once said, "The poorest man I know is the man who has nothing but money."

The following lyric was inspired by Proverbs 17:1: "Better is a dry morsel and quietness with it than a house full of feasting with strife." Perhaps the wealthy men we just mentioned understood that the truly important things in life cannot be bought with money.

Where I Live

I live in the shadow of a mountain
Where a rich man lives; he's got a fountain
And every hour at the gate
A policeman waits
To turn away the ones he ain't countin'.

I hear he's got his own gymnasium
And his precious art collection is amazing
But even with all of that
I've heard it's so sad
How much his children hate him.

I'd rather have a bite of bread
At a table where there's peace
Than to have all his trouble
At a table with a feast.

I'd rather live where I live
If love is here
Than to have a house full of treasures
And a heart full of tears.

Sometimes I see him at a distance
And there's always someone giving him assistance.
They open up his limo door
When they take him to the store.
They fly him in his jet to do business.

I've heard it's true but I never saw it
There's gold in his bathroom faucets.
He's got a helicopter pad
But even with all that
I heard his wife just came out of the closet.

I'd rather have a bite of bread
At a table where there's peace
Than to have all his trouble
At a table with a feast.

I'd rather live where I live
If love is here
Than to have a house full of treasures
And a heart full of tears.[3]

Content but Not Crazy

When contentment is missing in one or both spouses, the potential for conflict and ongoing financial stress is hard to avoid. Can we truly learn to be content and escape the vacuum of indebtedness that seeks to suck the life out of us and our marriages? We are given an encouraging example in the scriptures that assures us we can. The apostle Paul handled his dire circumstances as well as anyone we could recommend. Even though he found himself imprisoned in a Roman dungeon, he joyfully spoke of the freedom of gaining contentment in the heart. Through his writings to the church at Philippi, he shared the "key" to contentment. He wrote, "I know how to get along with humble means, and I also know how to live in prosperity; in any and every circumstance I have learned the secret of being filled and going hungry, both of having abundance and suffering need" (Philippians 4:12). What is that secret "key" to contentment? It's found in the very next verse, "I can do all things through [Christ] who strengthens me" (verse 13).

Philippians 4:13 is one of the most frequently quoted Bible verses among committed Christians. However, it is often referenced, not in the context of being content with what we have, but to give comfort and strength during other times of stress. For instance, perhaps you have found help from this verse when a hospital official called with the news that there had been an automobile accident and someone in your family was badly hurt. Or it could have been when the police called and said, "You need to come down here. We have your child in custody." It is at times like these, when our hearts are broken and our capacity to cope is exhausted, that we justifiably rely on the truth of this verse.

While it is fully appropriate to enlist the encouragement found in "I can do all things through [Christ] who strengthens me," don't forget the economic context of the verse. It is more than permissible to use it when your finances are in a "train wreck." It is especially then that we need to remember where our strength lies. And when we feel imprisoned by our appetites, and the temptation to spend ourselves into oblivion leaves us feeling hopeless and helpless, it is then that we must remember that "with Christ's help I can be content." Thankfully, we *can* say no to our lust for things. We can even find great satisfaction in sacrificing our wants in order to achieve our goal. How can we do that? Once again, we can do it because *we can do all things through Christ who strengthens us*.

Though we are confident that this is good advice, we must warn you that if you start trying to live your life free from the manic grab for more and more things, your friends and family may think you have lost your mind. Only a crazy person would put themselves in uncomfortable situations when "easy credit" makes all our wants so readily available. Why would anyone in their right mind do without in this day and age of "have it all, have it now, pay later," or, "take it home today, and no payments until 3004!!"

While our own personal quest for financial freedom has yielded great peace and happiness in our hearts, we know firsthand that attempting to live in contentment can be misunderstood as crazy. Yet we remained determined to stay out of debt, even if it meant being momentarily uncomfortable, inconvenienced, and ridiculed. For example, when we moved into our little house at the end of the summer in 1977 (the one with the incredibly beautiful basement steps), it was only a few weeks before the weather started to turn. It was then that we realized the house we had just bought didn't have an efficient source of heat. The little electric wall heaters that I had to turn on each time I wanted any warmth would have made our utility meter spin like a skill saw blade. It didn't take a rocket scientist to figure out that to pay the bill for warming our house with wall heaters would have required a government loan. Therefore, we made a deliberate decision to begin saving our money until we could pay cash to put in a central heating and cooling system.

In the interim we bought a free-standing Franklin wood-burner for $100. That was our only source of heat. Firewood was cheap and ashes were good for the garden. We were plenty warm.

It took us seven years of saving before we could pay, without borrowing, for the heating/cooling system. That was seven long years of being cold in the winter and hot and sticky in the summer. Was the sacrifice worth it? We have to say, "Yes!" Did our friends and family want to come over and visit when it was bitterly cold outside or blistering hot in the summer? Not really. The note we found on our kitchen table from a couple to whom we had loaned our house while we were away on a concert trip said it all. They arrived in late July and checked in at the "Chapman Inn." However, they didn't stay but one of the three nights they planned. Their note read, "Dear Steve & Annie, Air conditioning technology has advanced further than you realize. We've gone to a hotel!" We certainly felt the sting of their assessment of our little dwelling, but we knew that learning to be content and not going into debt had a price, and we were willing to pay it.

Our social life was sometimes affected by our self-imposed debt-free craze. For instance, there were times when our friends wanted to go out to eat after church. If the money wasn't there, we would bow out of the opportunity and, instead, go home and have whatever food was in the pantry. It may have seemed to our brothers and sisters that we were unduly hard on ourselves, but never did we consider it an act of martyrdom to do what was necessary to reach our goal. To us, it wasn't a big deal to say "not today." We've simply realized through the years that sacrifice is always part of any accomplishment that is considered worthwhile.

It is not our intent to gloat over the fact that we have lived debt-free for the past 15 years, and that we have learned firsthand the joy of Romans 13:8 and Proverbs 22:7. Instead, by sharing our success we hope to inspire you to discover the wonderful delight in contentment. The lyric that follows expresses both a warning to the one enslaved by debt and God's plan for gaining contentment.

All I Should Owe
I am the one who tied these strings
That run from my heart to the lenders
But I am the one who thought I needed these things
Lust makes it hard to remember.

That all I should owe is love
All I should owe is love
It's the only debt approved
By the Father above
All I should owe anyone is love.

For so long now I've been a slave
To the ones from whom I have borrowed
But there will be freedom when these debts are paid
But Lord come and lead me through this sorrow.

'Cause, all I should owe is love
All I should owe is love
It's the only debt approved
By the Father above
All I should owe is love.

I'm gonna think twice
I'm gonna be wise
How I spend my wages
'Cause it's written in the Pages
That...

All I should owe is love
It's the only debt approved
By the Father above
All I should owe is love.[4]

The love of money—and the longing for it—is a pit all married couples must strive to avoid. There's nothing wrong with providing sufficiently for our families. Making a living is necessary. However, when the emphasis is on "making a killing," often the casualties of that effort are our loved ones. We've seen many people who have followed after the all-mighty dollar end up like 1 Timothy 6 describes. They have been snared by the temptation of possessions. Chasing after "stuff" has resulted in them plunging into ruin and destruction. And, tragically, some have even wandered away from the faith because of financial disappointments. That hurt pierces their hearts. Once again, the deadly trap that catches some folks is their insatiable wanting and longing for money.

Don't let what happened to the couple in this song happen to you. Let this story serve as a warning to never trade your marriage for a dollar. It is worth far more!

The Good Years

They were poor but they were happy
Like newlyweds will be
She worked down at the market
He worked at his degree.

He'd tell her, "Someday, baby,
When I'm a wealthy man
I'll buy you lots of fine things"
And he'd sit and hold her hand.

In the good years
When all they had was each other to hold on to
In the good years
When holding each other was all they wanted to do
Oh, their love was true
In the good years.

Well, he got his education
It's hanging on his wall
They've got a big house now, with three cars
But they hardly talk at all.

He's up there in his office
Sometimes to near daylight
She lays awake and wishes
For the days when things were right.

In the good years
When all they had was each other to hold on to
In the good years
When holding each other was all they wanted to do
Oh, their love was true
In the good years.

Now, he buys her lots of fine things
Just like he said he would
And he thinks they make her happy
But she'd trade them if she could.

For the good years
When all they had was each other to hold on to
For the good years
When holding each other was all they wanted to do
Oh, what happened to
The good years.[5]

eight

Lead or Get Out
of the Way

As the moment to leave for the Sunday morning church service quickly approached, the challenge of feeding and dressing four little ones was left, once again, to the mother. The impatient, schedule-sensitive dad fidgeted with his car keys, looked at his watch, and stood at the front door. Eventually he began showing his frustration by throwing verbal spears at his wife. Quickly her temper flared.

Suddenly the frazzled mother threw her long, yet-to-be-brushed hair away from her face, turned to her impetuous husband, drew her word-bow and launched the sharpest arrow in her quiver. "Look, why don't we trade roles this morning. You get the kids ready, and I'll go sit in the car and blow the horn." Thud!

Perhaps one of the most emotionally dangerous battlefields known to humankind is in the average Christian home on any given Sunday morning. The hurried stress of getting everyone ready and presentable enough to go to a house of worship has been known to cause nasty verbal explosions. The resulting shrapnel of cutting remarks can wound feelings that are not quickly healed. And many times those wounds are hidden from fellow saints as the family enters the church doors.

The fact is, the Christian soldiers and soldierettes who engage in these "Sunday morning battles" really shouldn't be surprised that such spiritual turmoil would be generated by doing something as spiritually worthwhile as going to church together. First Peter 5:8 warns that "your adversary, the devil, prowls around like a roaring lion seeking someone to devour." Satan hates the followers of Christ and all they stand for. It's no wonder that the "author of confusion" would be present each time a family attempts anything holy. And there's a good reason for it!

In Revelation 12:1 we read, "And they overcame him [Satan] because of the blood of the Lamb and because of the word of their testimony." Take note of all that was *not* mentioned in that passage. Houses, cars, careers, successes, hobbies, dreams, and toys are conspicuously missing from the list of the weapons that can defeat Satan. The list includes only two items, and since the atoning, shed blood of Christ can never succumb to any of Satan's efforts to destroy it, the only possible weapon left for the devil to try to annihilate is the "word of [our] testimony." And when it comes to marriages, he knows that if he can inject a sufficient amount of confusion and hatred into husbands and wives, then he can extinguish the light that a family can be in a sin-darkened world. As a result, Satan will have managed to lessen the effectiveness of the kingdom of God. Thus, the reason for his deviant presence in the home at moments like "Sunday go to meetin' time!"

The Higher Purpose

Fortunately, through wise counsel from older couples in our circle of friends, we learned early on in our relationship that Satan indeed wants to render marriages useless and ineffective. For that reason we both agreed that we needed to submit ourselves to God's design for our union. We were aware that without organizing according to His plan, we would never know the joy of realizing our "higher purpose" as a couple. While providing good company for one another and procreating are certainly wonderful and even biblical benefits of a marriage, we wanted to know the greater potential. We desired to become a powerful spiritual force that could overcome the darkness around us and, ultimately, draw others to the light of Christ that shines on us in the way that Psalm 4:6 describes: "Many are saying, 'Who will show us any good?' Lift up the light of Your countenance upon us, O LORD!"

To find the scriptural order for effective spiritual leadership in a marriage, we didn't have to look any further than the familiar instructions found in Ephesians 5:22-28:

> Wives, be subject to your own husbands, as to the Lord. For the husband is the head of the wife, as Christ also is the head of the church, He Himself being the Savior of the body. But as the church is subject to Christ, so also the wives ought to be to their husbands in everything.
>
> Husbands, love your wives, just as Christ also loved the church and gave Himself up for her, so that He might sanctify her, having cleansed her by the washing of water with the word, that He might present to Himself the church in all her glory, having no spot or wrinkle or any such thing; but that she would be holy and blameless. So husbands ought also to love their own wives as their own bodies. He who loves his own wife loves himself.

In the face of the intensely "me" oriented culture that we lived in during our late teens and early twenties, this Ephesians passage challenged our young, independent spirits. Yet, as newlyweds we prayed for strength to submit to God's divine order of the husband at the helm of the home and the wife supporting his guidance. Honestly, it was not an easy adjustment.

Admittedly, as a mid-1970s couple, the Ephesians passage left us feeling rather conflicted. We felt the passage overwhelmed the husband and demeaned the wife. But thankfully, we had help. To assist us in understanding our marital roles and what they were supposed to look like, an elderly husband, who had been a Tennessee Volunteers fan since the color orange was invented, compared a good marriage to three specific football team members. In his southern drawl, he said, "First of all, ya'll need to understand that the Lord is the coach. He calls all the shots. The quarterback is the husband. But that quarterback ain't worth a dime if he's not willing to listen to the coach *and*...if he doesn't have a sure-handed receiver, that is, a good wife. When she's willing to play the game the way it was designed, she can always make a quarterback look good!"

Even though we lean toward the blue-and-gold colors of our original home state team, the West Virginia Mountaineers, we agree with the man's sage advice. Without a doubt, the gridiron analogy that compares a quarterback and a receiver to the husband and wife holds enormous wisdom, and, though it might not be original, we will utilize it in this chapter. This picture can contribute as much as any other to the spiritual health, effectiveness, and success of a marriage.

We asked wives to respond to the following question: "In what ways has your husband been a spiritual leader to you and your family?" Even though the women gave a variety of answers, there was one thread that seemed to run through most of their replies. Many of the wives indicated that their husbands' spiritual leadership was very crucial to them. Here are some of the many responses we received:

- Even though my husband is a faithful church-goer, he compartmentalizes his religion to Sundays. He doesn't want to be involved in any other way.

- My husband makes his decisions based on God's Word. There's one major problem: He doesn't study and know God's Word. It's really just a show.

- My husband is very involved with mission projects and has led the way for our children to see the importance of helping. However, having a devotional time at home has been a weak place in our family.

- Even though my husband has no interest in church or my church family, I appreciate that he has never tried to stop me or the children from attending services.

- My husband is really trying to be the spiritual leader in our family. We have prayer each night before we eat dinner. He reads his Bible and weaves God's Word into our family conversations. My only source of frustration is his unwillingness for us to go away for spiritual renewal weekends, just the two of us.

- My husband is the pastor so, of course, we go to church each Sunday. However, at home we don't pray together, God's Word is not read, and he spends most of his free time on the computer, playing online games. He neglects my daughter and me.

- I appreciate that my husband has always tithed and supported our church.

* I long for a worship time in our home with my husband's involvement.

* My husband is a good example to my unsaved extended family. They always ask him to pray when there's an occasion that is appropriate. He prays for my family in private. I love that!

* My husband has no time for the things of the Lord. His Sunday mornings are used for things he wants to do.

* He has just recently renewed his commitment to the Lord. However, it's really hard for him to be consistent as a leader in our family.

* I'm the spiritual leader in our family, not my husband. He's a good follower and goes along with whatever I want to do, but he doesn't initiate it.

* He takes us to church, but I don't see any depth in his relationship with God. His prayers are shallow.

* I feel we are not spiritually connected or healthy enough for the full-time ministry load he feels he is called to. Time away from each other has caused the spiritual aspect of our relationship to suffer.

* My husband takes an authoritarian attitude that is harsh and rigid when it comes to God's Word and prayer. I'd rather he not lead at all if he's going to use that place as a hammer on me and the children.

* He thinks because I have more knowledge about God's Word that means he's unable to lead and contribute. I don't feel that way at all.

* My husband is consistent in church and out of church. He is a wonderful example to our children and the youth of our church.

* Every morning, no matter what's going on, we have prayer before we leave for the day.

- My husband does a good job as spiritual leader, as long as I prod him along. He is not self-motivated.

- He is a godly example to the whole family. He makes time to be with the Lord alone as well as with the rest of the family. What really gives him the leadership role is his successful attempts to control his anger. He treats me and the children in a very positive and loving way.

- My husband is wonderful to pray and talk with the children each night before they go to sleep. He doesn't do as well having that spiritual relationship with me.

- It was my husband who got me started going to church. He is our spiritual leader in every way.

- I think our kids would listen to my husband if he would talk to them about the Lord. I try, but they shut me out.

- When I was at a spiritually low point in my life, it was my husband who kept encouraging me to read, pray, and get back into church.

- I feel more like the leader in our family. I need my husband to know that this is my number-one need, and he's not meeting it.

- It has been difficult teaching my children how to live a godly life and then trying to counteract what their daddy says and does.

- I have literally begged him to lead our family spiritually. He knows how but refuses to do what is right.

- He saw to it that we had our devotions together on our honeymoon night, and every night since then. (Married 48 years)

- We're leaders in our church, but we have no spiritual, devotional time at home together.

- My husband reads his Bible and the children see this. He is the "watchman on the wall." However, when his tongue gets away from him and he starts cussing, I wonder what this says to the children.

Equal Time

Several of the wives revealed their sincere thanks for a "quarterback" who could lead their team down the field of life. However, as you probably saw, many of them were not subtle with their frustrations over feeling like they could face a loss due to their "passer" not having enough leadership skills or sufficient interest in even being in the game. But the women represent only one side of the coin. On the other side are the husbands who were very forthright in expressing the difficulty they felt in adequately leading the spiritual life of their marriages and families. When the men were asked, "What is your greatest challenge when it comes to being the spiritual leader in your family?" they did not hold back.

- If my wife wants me to be the leader of the family, then she needs to step back and let me try. As long as she is doing it, why should I?

- Whenever I try to pray with my family or lead in any kind of Bible study, my wife keeps interrupting me.

- My job takes me away from home. It's hard to establish any kind of routine when I don't know when I'll be home.

- It's hard for me to take on the spiritual leadership because I know my life is not that consistent. I don't want to come off like a hypocrite to my family.

- It's hard to feel like a leader in my family. My wife doesn't support me in decisions that have nothing to do with our spiritual life. I feel undercut before I even start.

- My prayer life really lacks. I feel guilty when I try to come off like some spiritual giant.

- Having teenage kids can throw a wrench in trying to have family devotions.

- I find it very difficult to pray out loud.

* My wife tries to help me, but I find it tough to find the time to talk about God and pray with my family.

* I don't read very well, and I feel self-conscious when I try to lead the family in Bible study.

* I don't know enough about the Bible to even think about teaching it. I'd come off really stupid.

* We don't have a great relationship as a couple. I don't feel like she trusts me or respects my values. This doesn't really set a very good mood for devotions.

* When I try to lead my family spiritually, I come across as demanding. Have you ever tried to get kids to sit still for devotions? I don't want to do it if I end up yelling at them to listen to me.

* I simply don't have enough time to do it.

* I guess I feel like the devil keeps me from being the leader I should be.

* My biggest challenge is living the way I tell my children to live. It's hard to be the kind of example I want to be: loving, merciful, and forgiving.

* I don't really hear God's voice. It's hard to teach what you don't know.

* I'm not really consistent in my own quiet time. I suppose that's why I'm not consistent with our family devotions.

* I struggle to stay away from sexual temptations. That interferes with leading my family.

* My wife and I don't agree on some beliefs. It's just easier to stay away from the controversy.

* I know my wife wants me to be the spiritual leader more than anything in our marriage. I just need to take the time to make it happen.

* My temper is the biggest hindrance to being a spiritual leader.

- Making sure I live an obedient life to God is my greatest challenge.

- I don't read enough on the subject.

- Starting something and sticking to it is tough.

- My wife is the spiritual leader in our family, but I'm trying.

- Just physically getting everyone in the same room seems impossible.

- My greatest challenge is treating my wife in a positive way that will affect my children for the good.

- I know what's right, I just don't know how to lead.

- My faith is not as strong as my wife's.

- I need my wife to tell me that she's praying for me, and then I need her to do it.

- I don't have a relationship with God. I leave that to my wife.

- Somehow it's hard for me to remember to take things to God first, before they get out of hand.

- Even when I lead, I don't feel like my family is following me.

From the honest input of both the "quarterbacks" and the "receivers," it is safe to say that what husbands and wives are not saying about leadership is:

Wives: "It is very important to me that our family have effective spiritual leadership. If you will not do the job, then I suppose I will have to do it myself. That's not what I want, but the spiritual health of our home is dependent on it, and it is too crucial to leave undone."

Husbands: "I know I should be the spiritual leader of our home, but I don't know how, and I don't feel equipped or worthy of the job. But if you want me to lead, then you must step aside and let me try."

If either of these statements describes your feelings, perhaps the following suggestions will provide some guidance on how to become a winning team.

Our Game Plan

By revealing the way our little team has operated, we have a sincere hope that our game plan might benefit you. For that reason, we offer the three most important contributing factors that have helped us gain precious yardage against the opposition by becoming better followers of Christ and leaders in the family. They are: *God's Word, prayer,* and *fellowship with believers.*

God's Word

The Bible, God's holy word, is the complete resource center for any team. It contains the rules for the game, which must be studied and understood. It also has the necessary equipment that must be issued and faithfully worn. And, unlike any other team manual that exists, His word provides the power that can change a player from one who may be mediocre in skills to one who has abilities that can surpass even his own expectations.

Steve: I am personally grateful for these unique characteristics of God's Word. In it I have found hope as a husband/leader who sometimes feels inadequate in my ability to guide my family. Hebrews 4:12 offers me this encouragement:

> For the word of God is living and active and sharper than any two-edged sword, and piercing as far as the division of soul and spirit, of both joints and marrow, and able to judge the thoughts and intentions of the heart.

And Psalm 119:98-104 will strengthen any "quarterback" who hesitates to get into the game:

> Thy commandments make me wiser than my enemies.... I have more insight than all my teachers, for Your testimonies are my meditation. I understand more than the aged, because I have observed Your precepts. I have restrained my feet from every evil way, that I may keep Your word. I have not turned aside from Your ordinances,

for You Yourself have taught me....From Your precepts I
get understanding.

To illustrate how God's Word can have a positive effect on a man's
ability and willingness to step forward and take the lead, consider this
true, but painful story.

Several years ago we had an office that housed a few employees, one
of whom was given the responsibility of representing us to the public.
One month, when the telephone bills came, I carefully screened them,
as I normally did, for any unusual charges that should not be listed. That's
when I discovered an unfamiliar business had been called from our
office. Upon further investigation, I learned that the number was actually connected to a "phone porn" line and had been called from a particular number in our system.

While I am not one who is comfortable at all with confrontation and
tend to avoid it any time I can, I approached the employee with the
results of my probe. Confessions followed, and I presented a warning that
if it occurred once more he would be released immediately. Unfortunately, the illicit phone calls were made again. Sadly, that which I had
dreaded to do had to be done. Enter Annie!

My sweet wife, who is, by nature, not always as hesitant as I am to
let the chips fall where they may, begged for mercy on behalf of the
employee. A house full of young children depended on the person's
income and, worse yet, the confrontation came right in the midst of the
Christmas season. Feeling pity for that family, Annie pleaded for his job.
However, in my desperation to know God's will for the situation, I had
gone to His written word for wisdom.

What I found in the pages was some clear direction regarding the
employee. First of all, I have always been a strong proponent of maintaining a good name. The Proverbs 22:1 passage is, as far as I'm concerned, much more than a nicely worded quip. It is a mandate: "A
good name is to be more desired than great wealth...."

Even though it meant firing the person who was jeopardizing the
"good name" I had tried to preserve over the years, I had to be willing
to follow through. In addition, 1 Corinthians 5:9-13 provided the necessary muscle my weak soul would need to keep my promise. Paul
instructed:

I wrote you in my letter not to associate with immoral people; I did not at all mean with the immoral people of this world, or with the covetous and swindlers, or with idolaters, for then you would have to go out of the world. But actually, I wrote to you not to associate with any so-called brother if he is an immoral person, or covetous, or an idolater, or a reviler, or a drunkard, or a swindler—not even to eat with such a one. For what have I to do with judging outsiders? Do you not judge those who are within the church? But those who are outside, God judges. Remove the wicked man from among yourselves.

Based on the authority of the scripture and an unyielding desire to maintain a good name, I did what I had to do. I fired the employee. It was a painful time for us all, perhaps more for the person fired than me. Still, for the sake of protecting our reputation from the negative publicity that could have resulted, the deed was done...even though I had to go against the grain of my personality to do it. As it turned out, the phone bill investigation trail that I followed led me to discover that had I not dismissed the employee when I did, there would be other waves of deception that could have cost us our credibility. Thanks be to God for the power and authority of His word to guide us personally into righteousness. He can help us rightly guide others, especially our mates, through the maze of spiritual opposition.

Annie: I can say without reservation that I fully embrace my role as the "pass receiver" in our marriage. I do so because I have come to understand the biblical design for the function of a wife. However, that understanding did not come without much resistance.

Not long after I became a Christian, and before we married, I started faithfully reading and studying God's word. However, the more I read my Bible, the more I realized there was an obvious problem. God and I didn't think alike—an attitude that was described in Isaiah 55:8: " 'For My thoughts are not your thoughts, nor are your ways My ways,' declares the LORD."

To be perfectly honest, there were parts of the scriptures that made me absolutely furious. I could hardly contain myself when I read, for example, the passages concerning how husbands and wives were to relate to one another. There was no doubt about it—something had to change!

Since God made it clear, long before I was ever on the scene that He does not change (Malachi 3:6) and neither do His words (Matthew 24:35; Luke 16:17; Mark 13:31), I was left with only one sensible decision. It was a simple choice, but just because it wasn't complicated didn't make it any easier.

The root of my intellectual wrestling match with God was due partly to growing into my young adult years in the 1960s. I had been exposed to, and consequently embraced, some of the most vicious of the feminist ideas of the time. Actually, when it was all boiled down, I had developed a great disdain and hatred for men and children. That was not my only point of disagreement, but it was a significant factor. It wasn't, however, until God's truth began to permeate my reasoning that I began to realize just how far off track I was.

Diagnosing the problem was an important part of my progression toward getting on the same page with God. The next logical conclusion was that my errant thinking had to be corrected. Interestingly enough, the only solution to my dilemma was found in the very book that gave me pause. Just as we quoted earlier from the book of Hebrews, God's word is "living and sharper than any two-edged sword." In fact, I read that the kind of two-edged sword mentioned in this passage was able to pierce through the strongest armor. My entire heart, mind, and soul was shrouded in a thick, protective shield made of the metal of "self." Only God's word would be able to cut through it and set me free to right thinking.

In order to accomplish the tough task of getting my mind to agree with God, I began to wake up early each morning and diligently study the truths contained in the Bible. Knowing that my "flesh" would not quickly comply to its teachings, I particularly targeted those passages that gave me the most trouble.

Slowly I began to see a change take place in me. It was as though I could hardly recognize myself. Not only did I begin to see the truth in God's word intellectually, but my behavior and personality also began to improve. Where, for instance, my reaction to the role of a wife might have been expressed in hot anger and sharp words, after a time of His refining through His word I noticed I began to offer more of a softened and kinder response. The number-one benefactor of this transformation has been my "quarterback"! I can honestly say, now, that I love it when he "throws me a pass"!

Prayer

Steve: Along with the enormous value of God's word that can help us be leaders, and be led, prayer is also of utmost importance. In football terms, if scripture is the divine "play book," then prayer is similar to what the players do when they run to the sidelines to consult with the coach.

It is an undeniable imperative that a quarterback, for example, who might not be clear on what the next move may be, call a time-out and connect with his leader. There, he takes a few moments to ask for direction, ask for help, and even to reassure himself that he is correctly following the game plan. When he returns to the family he is leading downfield, he displays more confidence and in turn, the entire team (wife and children) can take comfort in his poise. But as valuable as prayer is to my role as leader, I admit there are times when I have struggled to enlist that piece of equipment. My best illustration of this fault came early in my relationship with Annie, even before we said our vows in marriage.

It was just a month or two prior to our March 1975 wedding day when we were traveling in our old 1950 Chevy on our way to church. About three miles from the sanctuary, the old car suddenly lost forward power. The engine continued to run fine, so I knew right away that the transmission had failed. I drifted off to the side of the road and turned the motor off. Annie sat next to me, and listened as I mumbled my grumbles. "I'm gonna have to walk back to that gas station in the rain. I can't believe this!" Two or three very long minutes passed as I mentally prepared to melt in the pouring rain.

I was about to exit the car and go for help when Annie put her left hand out as if she wanted me to hold it.

"What?" I asked.

"Let's pray for Sarah." (That was the name we had given the old Chevy. We named her that because she was like Sarah in the Bible... old and still productive!)

It's at this part of the story that I reveal how slow I can be to enlist the power of prayer. As Annie held her hand out waiting for me to decide whether or not to take it, I immediately felt two emotions. One, I felt embarrassed and guilty that I had not been the first to think of taking our car crisis to our caring Father in heaven. I somehow knew I should have been the leader with that action. Second, I felt a little resentful that she had not given me time enough to think of it myself. Of course, we might still be there today if she had waited on me. Though my ego was a little wounded, I chose to take her hand while saying, "I'll pray!" (It was the least I could do.)

Having never prayed for a car before, I stumbled through my opening remarks to the Lord. "Father, I've…never prayed for a car before…'cause up to this point I've driven Fords!" [Actually I didn't add the Ford part, but the rest is accurate.] I continued with a prayer that went something like this, "Father, would You please touch Sarah. She's terribly sick and is in need of a miracle. We're on our way to church. [I thought a few brownie points might help.] We ask You to do this for us in Jesus' name. Amen."

To be honest, as I prayed I didn't sense a fiery volcano of faith erupting in my soul. It felt more like the flicker of a damp kitchen match. Still, I had managed to lead my bride-to-be in one of our very first prayers in time of crisis. I did feel good about that.

I turned the power key back to the "on" position with my left hand, and then I let go of her hand and pushed the little, silver ignition button on the dash to start the engine. The motor quickly came alive and seemed to purr in anticipation of leaving the lonely spot on the road. My heart pounded with excitement as I pushed in the clutch, and my hand nearly shook with expectancy as I pulled the shifter down into first gear. We both knew that the moment of truth was only seconds away.

Slowly I pressed the gas pedal and began to release the clutch. Would Sarah move forward? Had God really heard our little prayer? We were about to find out.

Suddenly, I felt the old girl's transmission tighten and respond to the accelerator. I didn't hardly have time to look back as Sarah shot out onto the highway. All I could do was hold on and shout, "Hallelujah!"

We were convinced we had just seen a miracle. We giggled with joy. And because of the level of faith that instantly swelled up in my heart, I seriously considered seizing the moment by praying, "Lord, while You're at it, heal the play in this steering wheel!" I don't remember if I went that far or not.

That particular prayer was prayed only once in our marriage. It yielded a miracle we had not seen before nor have we seen one like it since. It was unique for the hour. Why did God bless us in that moment in 1975? I think I know the answer. God wanted a young husband-to-be to know that prayer is a mighty tool that He has graciously given and can be used with liberality. Matthew 18:19 can be a precious hope to a "prayer bashful" husband. These amazing words come straight from the lips of Christ: "Again I say to you, that if two of you agree on the earth about anything that they may ask, it shall be done for them by My Father who is in heaven." What a marvelous promise!

By the way, have you ever considered why on earth it would be true that "if two of you agree...it shall be done"? Very simply, it is nothing less than a miracle when two people agree on anything. I think God's attention is captured when two stubborn, self-willed human beings find unanimity. My hesitation to agree with Annie about our old, sick Chevy is a case in point.

My heart of "flesh" did not want to respond to the urging of the Holy Spirit as I sat beside my sweetheart. But oh, how glad I am that I did. Truthfully, I am saddened by the thought of what I could have caused us to miss on that day in 1975. It would have been beyond tragic had I allowed my guilt, embarrassment, and feelings of inadequacy to hinder me from taking Annie's hand and agreeing with her in prayer. What a sad loss of a valuable lesson it would have been!

Even with that incredibly encouraging moment in our history to recall, I still struggle to this day with being immediately willing to pray with my wife. One very good reason that I sometimes balk is because she knows me so well...and God knows me even better. Though I believe they each deeply love me, to be in the presence of both God and Annie at the same time is, to say the least, rather uncomfortable. She sees me when I get upset, for example, and act foolishly. And for sure, God is always watching. Because of that, I am tempted to shut down and remain silent. Yet, I have seen the power of prayer and have learned that I have to be willing to set aside my feelings of shame and humbly bow on the knees of my heart. When I do make that choice, I am never, ever disappointed. Neither is Annie. Neither is the Lord, according to Psalm 86:5: "For You, Lord, are good and ready to forgive, and abundant in lovingkindness to all who call upon You." Invariably, praying *with* Annie to our Father in heaven has been the right thing to do, but admittedly, not the easiest.

I must add this encouragement to husbands who may also struggle as I do with the awkwardness of praying with your wife. As you "practice" praying together, it will be easier to add the children who will either come along later or who may already be under your roof. Keep in mind that praying *with* your kids can be quite different than praying *for* them. When our children were small, it was always tempting to let our prayer time with them be swept under the rug of busyness. Yet, when we stayed true to the important opportunity to teach them the power of prayer, some very memorable things would happen. Heidi, for example, was just three or four years old when we were praying with her one night. We were offering up the Lord's Prayer. When we got to one familiar line in the prayer she said, "Deliver us from *eagles!*" Then she looked up, furrowed her brow, and announced, *"I hate eagles!"* For some reason she had a fear of the mighty bird. As it turned out, we never had a problem with our national bird around our house.

Another unforgettable event happened with Nathan and prayers. He came to me one day in his fourth year and said, "Dad, I want a set of drums." He had been inspired by a drummer whom he'd seen perform with a band at our church. My response was one of self-defense for my hearing more than anything. I said (truthfully), "Son, we can't afford to buy you a set of drums. Why don't you ask God if He will give you a set?" I felt safe that our home would miss the rattling of our floors. However, I had not counted on God being so willing to answer the prayers of a child.

In just a few days a fellow approached Nathan at church and, without knowing about his petition, asked, "Nathan, would you like to have some drums?" You could have mopped me up off the floor with a sponge. I gathered my wits and immediately dropped to one knee and whispered in Nathan's little, innocent ear, "Son, we need a van!" I figured if he had that kind of connection, why not take advantage of it.

While praying with children can yield for them life-changing lessons about God's ability to answer our cries, praying with your wife for your children is equally important. Furthermore, it ought to be done with fervor and with regularity. We often lift our children's names up to the Lord throughout the week, but we have also chosen Wednesdays to concentrate our prayers for them. The following lyric is called "Wednesday's Prayer." It contains many of the desires we have in our hearts for our two, now-grown children, Nathan and Heidi. Their spouses, Stephanie and Emmitt, have since been added to the list.

Wednesday's Prayer

Father God, to you I come
In the name of your Son
I bring my children to your throne
Father hear my cry.

Above all else, Lord save their souls
Draw them near you; keep them close
Be the shield against their foes
Make them yours, not mine.

Give them peace in Christ alone
In their sorrow, be their song
No other joy will last as long
Father calm their fears.

Guide their feet, Lord, light their path
May their eyes on you be cast
Give their hands a kingdom task
A purpose for their years.

And when my flesh cries out for bread
May I hunger, Lord, instead
That my children would be fed
On your words of life.

So, Father God, to you I come
In the name of your Son
I bring my children to your throne
Father, hear my cry.[1]

The lines in the lyric aren't the only things we call on the Lord about in regard to our kids. I'll never forget the night Annie and I were backstage before a concert. We had worded the above prayer for Nathan and Heidi who were, at the time, single and in college. At the end of our prayer Annie added, "And Lord, wherever they are, whatever they're doing... make 'em stop!" It was sort of a "catch all" measure that I thought was quite fitting in the face of having only a very short time to pray.

Annie: As an encouragement to wives who long for their men to get involved in leading their family in prayer, consider the woman I talked to who had been married for more than 20 years. In our conversation she relayed some fears she dealt with prior to her wedding day. She said, "I was praying and I said to the Lord, 'Father, I'm not sure the man I am about to marry is the spiritual leader he needs to be. I always thought I would marry someone more spiritually mature than he seems to be.'" She continued, "God then spoke to my heart and whispered, 'If you will be faithful to pray for him, just wait and see what I can do with your husband.' That day I determined that I would never nag him about his spiritual responsibilities. Instead, I committed to pray for him." As it turned out, her husband is one of the strongest and most effective spiritual leaders in a home that we have seen. Prayer really does change things—and husbands, too!

One final note to support the need for praying as a family. We asked our friends Lindsey and Susan to discuss with us the importance of prayer in their family. Susan eagerly said, "Prayer is *the* most important part of our relationship and has been since the beginning of our marriage. Before we had children I worked outside the home. Each morning, before Lindsey and I parted for the day, the two of us prayed together. I can't fully express the significance of that simple prayer. But what made it even more special to me, was the fact it was Lindsey who initiated it. Somehow, I felt close to him all day long because of the spiritual unity promoted by taking a few minutes to commit our day, and each other, to the Lord.

"Then," she continued, "when we had our children, it was just a natural part of our life." She then added her hopes that we would pass the following advice to newlyweds. "If you will, please encourage young couples to start, from the very beginning of their marriage to at least pray together every day. It will change everything about their relationship. It will make every aspect better."

Then Lindsey noted, "Our children would really be upset if we tried to skip our evening, bedtime ritual. What we do is not that big of a deal. It honestly takes just a few minutes...minutes we all enjoy. We read a Bible story together, sing a song, and each of us takes turns praying. It's as much a part of our evening routine as brushing our teeth before we go to bed. We wouldn't even think of not doing it.

"Our hope," he continued, "is as the children get older and enter into the challenging teen years, it won't seem so unusual to get them to have family devotions with us."

Our friends' efforts as a husband/wife, mom/dad team is an example that is a worthy one to follow. But Lindsey and Susan also admitted to us that while their method worked great for them, they had friends who did it differently. There is no set formula for accomplishing the high goal of having consistent family devotions. The important act is simply to do it, even when it is difficult. Besides, leading the family in devotions can lead to some wonderful, precious moments.

Precious Moments

Our days have been filled with times to remember
We've had moments with tears and moments with laughter
But the time has not ended in this day God has loaned us
What will we do with these few precious moments?

I'll call the children, and I'll get the letter
Before we're lost in our sleep, we'll gather together
And read from the heart of the God who has saved us
And kneel for a while in His presence.

And these will be precious moments in His presence
It's the best time we'll ever spend
Our family's devoted to
These precious moments with Him.

Well, the children are busy, there are things I must do
It seems so hard to carry it through
But it's always this way; it's always a fight
But let's not be defeated tonight.

For these will be precious moments in His presence
It's the best time we'll ever spend
Our family's devoted
To these precious moments with Him.[2]

Fellowship with Believers

Returning once again to the picture of a marriage found on the football field, specifically in the quarterback and receiver, it is necessary to note how often the two of them gather in a huddle with the rest of the team during a game. Very simply, a husband and wife desperately need to gather often with their spiritual family, their local congregation. The benefits of "huddling at church" with the rest of the players is clearly described in Hebrews 10:23-25: "Let us hold fast the confession of our hope without wavering, for He who promised is faithful; and let us consider how to stimulate one another to love and good deeds, not forsaking our own assembling together, as is the habit of some, but encouraging one another; and all the more, as you see the day drawing near."

Steve: One of the best examples of how valuable it is to gather with others of like mind is found in the admonition to men written in 2 Timothy 2:22: "Now flee from youthful lusts and pursue righteousness, faith, love and peace, with those who call on the Lord from a pure heart." According to this verse, there are three distinct actions that are necessary in order to find victory over lust. It is clear that not only must a man *flee* from the temptation, he must also *pursue*, or run to, Christ, our only source of righteousness, faith, love, and peace. But note that a man who wants to overcome a battle with lust should add one other action. He should do so *with others* who embrace the same goal.

God, in His great wisdom, knows that men need to "huddle" with their spiritual family. It is during these gatherings that, as the Hebrews 10 passage reveals, we spur one another to a closer walk with Christ, thus, helping us to be better individuals and better mates. In turn, we can lead our families to become brighter lights in our dark world.

Annie: Just as important as it is for men to connect with other men at church, it is equally essential for women to find support and friendship with like-minded sisters in Christ. There are some issues that women grapple with that only another woman can truly understand. Even though a husband may be sympathetic to her struggles, there are some challenges, like the stress of motherhood and physical changes, that are unique to females. It is very often that comfort and good guidance can be found only in the company of other sisters.

May God bless you as you lead and follow.

nine

A Regret-Free Marriage

For a period of time we traveled to our marriage seminars with, of all things, a set of handcuffs in our luggage. Sound strange? As a matter of fact, it *felt* strange the day we forgot to put them in our checked bags and instead had mistakenly put them in our carry-on. We were sternly queried at the security checkpoint by a government official. Especially since September 11, 2001, trying to take questionable items such as handcuffs onto a plane can be misconstrued as rather threatening. As the security officers suspiciously glared at us, we were left to do a verbal tap-dance. We tried to explain why we would need handcuffs in our marriage conference meetings. Eventually, the authorities allowed us to take the cuffs back to the ticket counter and place them in a separate box. They were then put underneath with the other checked bags.

You might be wondering, even as the airport security personnel were, why in this world we would be carrying handcuffs with us to our seminars designed to encourage married couples to love one another. The reason is quite simple. The shackles were used to illustrate the sad truth that as long husbands or wives are "locked up" with regrets from the past, they are incapable of reaching out and offering love to the other. People who are chained with remorse are usually rendered emotionally paralyzed.

Everyone has experienced regrets at sometime in his or her life. Sadly enough, they seem to be part of the cold realization that we all do things we wish we hadn't done or fail to do things we should have. Nonetheless, if we allow regrets to keep our focal point on the past, we are setting ourselves up for trouble. Someone once said that living with your focus on regrets is like trying to drive your car while looking in the rearview mirror; there's no doubt about it—you're going to crash!

We asked wives to share some of the regrets they harbored. They indicated that these feelings have affected their personal lives, and, in some instances, have had a derogatory impact on their marriages.

- I wish I could have stayed home with my children. I feel like they grew up, and I didn't have enough time with them.

- I wish my husband and I wouldn't have fought and argued in front of the children.

- I regret trying to cover up my husband's mistakes. I'm finally having to tough it out and let the chips fall where they need to. I'm exhausted trying to make it all better for him.

- I'm afraid we got married too soon. We were counseled to wait, but we didn't.

- If I could change anything in my marriage, I would have spoken up and made myself be heard. Keeping quiet didn't help either of us.

- I wish I would have known God's word better and taught it to my children. I regret not spending more quality time and having more intimate conversations about God's plan for a pure and moral life with my children.

- I wish we would have chosen to be married in a church instead of having a garden wedding. It was our second marriage, and I think we needed the spiritual influence that a church wedding would have given. I think it would have set a better tone for the two sets of children who were being blended into one family.

- I cleaned house and worked instead of playing and talking to my children. This is one thing I definitely would change if I could.

- I wish we would have tried harder to have family devotions.

* I wish my husband would have been a Christian.

* My husband is consumed with pornography. I hate the way it makes me feel when I'm with him. It has definitely hurt our marriage.

* We raised our children in a legalistic, judgmental church. We later made the change, but not soon enough for our older children.

* I wish we had not lived together before we got married.

* I wish we had had more time to think about what marriage was going to be like before we got married. I was pregnant, and so everything just kind of happened.

* I regret not teaching my sons how to do more around the house (cooking, cleaning, doing their own laundry).

* If I could change one thing, I would have asked Jesus into my life sooner. My husband and I were not Christians when we got married. I regret the wasted years.

* We should have moved away from the people who were a bad influence on us.

* I regret not making "our relationship" more of a priority over the children. Now that the kids are older, I feel like my husband and I don't really know each other.

* I wish I had not yelled at my family when I got upset. If I could change that, I would.

* I regret not going to college. It would have helped more if I could have carried more of the financial load.

* I regret having had an abortion. I get really upset when anyone talks about the subject. Even though I'm a Christian, if the topic is brought up at church, I leave. I know it's wrong; I just don't want to hear about it.

* I wish I had had more fun with my kids and more time with my husband.

* We should have set up rules in our household before our children were teenagers.

- We should never have moved close to his parents.

- I regret not teaching my daughters how to keep house. I spoiled them and did all the work they should have been doing. I've left them at a disadvantage.

- We should have changed the way we conducted our financial situation. We are so far in debt, I don't think we'll ever be financially secure.

- Even though I didn't work outside of the home, and I would have called myself a "stay-at-home" mom, I never really stayed at home. I ran too much with volunteer work, errands, shopping, and so on....I didn't do the job at home that I could have or should have done.

- I wish my husband and I would have prayed together. Whenever we would hear someone preach about having a prayer time as a couple, we would talk about it but never followed through. I feel like something is missing between us as a result.

- We should have found a church we *both* liked. As a result of not agreeing on a church, we were never as active and faithful to our church as we should have been. I fear, as a result of us not locking into faithful attendance, our children never seemed to connect to the idea.

- Early in our marriage, I gave all the power of decision making to my husband. In a way, I gave away my sense of self. I have regretted and resented him for that.

- I moved into my husband's house that he shared with his first wife. I should have cleared out all of her stuff prior to marrying him.

- I regret never really enjoying my children. I wanted them to grow up quickly. They kept me from doing things I wanted to do, got in my way, and drove me crazy. Looking back, I feel foolish for being so short sighted. I wish I could do some of it over.

❧ I regret never being satisfied with the way I look. I always thought I was so fat and unattractive. But now, when I see pictures that were taken a few years ago, I think, "I looked great!" My husband tried to tell me he thought I was beautiful, but I wouldn't believe him. I've wasted a lot of time hating myself.

The husbands also shared some of their regrets and how focusing on them has hurt them personally as well as their marriages.

❧ I regret raising our children in a spiritually unfit environment.

❧ I feel badly that my wife and I fought and argued in front of the children.

❧ I regret buying a house that was too large for our income. The financial stress is suffocating me. I feel the pressure all the time.

❧ If I could change anything, I would have been a nicer person to live with. I regret being so harsh and mean to my wife and kids.

❧ I wish I had not had an affair and betrayed my wife.

❧ I regret hitting my wife.

❧ I wish we hadn't lived together before we got married.

❧ Sometimes I treated my wife mean, just to make myself look important.

❧ I regret straying away from church.

❧ We got married too young. If I could go back, I would have waited until we were more grown-up and mature.

❧ I regret emotionally disconnecting with my wife and kids.

❧ I let anger dominate me.

❧ I guess I've been really selfish. I bought a lot of "toys" (boats, trucks, video games) that put financial stress on us.

❧ I regret not saving sex for my wife.

- If I could change anything, I would not have made such a big deal out of small stuff. If the house wasn't perfect, I gave my wife a hard time. I look back now and realize I should helped her keep it clean instead of yelling at her.

- I wish I hadn't had to work so many hours. Now my kids are grown and gone, and I don't really know them.

- I regret buying whatever I wanted.

- I wish I hadn't given up on my first marriage.

- I regret not finishing college. I've been limited in my career because I lacked a degree. I know more than the others around me, but they get the promotions.

- I regret not becoming a Christian sooner.

- I regret that I didn't finish high school.

- My wife had to work and leave the children in day care. I know she felt guilty and cheated of time with our kids. It couldn't be helped, though, 'cause I'm disabled. Just because there's a good reason doesn't make it any less disappointing.

- I regret that we didn't have more children. We've enjoyed the two we have so much, and at the time thought that's all we wanted, but now I wonder if we made the right decision.

- I've struggled with a pornography addiction for as long as I can remember. I regret the wasted time I've spent fantasizing and lusting over other women. I try to fight it, but it's really a battle.

- I know I'm gone too much from home by working. But when you have four children, how do you spend time with them and still work enough to keep everything going?

- I regret not sacrificing more when we were younger in order to save for retirement. The time is almost on us, and we are not ready. I don't know what we're going to do when I can't work anymore.

- It makes me sad when I think about how much my wife and I have drifted apart. We rarely have sex anymore.

- I wish I had been nicer to my family. Sometimes I wonder what they are going to remember about me when I'm gone.

- I regret that my second marriage isn't as happy as I thought it would be.

- I regret not having a good relationship with my dad. No matter what I've tried, he isn't there for me.

- I don't know if I will ever get over my wife's unfaithfulness.

- I backed the car over my little daughter. She died. I live with regrets every day.

- I regret getting my wife pregnant before we got married.

- I wish I hadn't done drugs and got in trouble when I was young. It's hard to tell my kids what to do when I did so many things I shouldn't have done.

- I regret leaving my first wife. It's done and I can't change it. I love my second wife, but sometimes I wonder what would have happened if we'd worked a little harder at the first marriage.

What can we conclude that husbands and wives aren't telling each other about the pain from their past is:

> "I love you and want to show you how I feel. However, there's a part of me that can't reach out to you because I am holding on to merciless regrets. My emotional paralysis has nothing to do with what you have done. I am the one who must deal with the pain from my past. As you pray for me and support my pursuit of God, I am confident I will find peace."

As we scanned the previous list by the husbands and wives we realized that all of their regrets could be resolved using three remedies...

Avoid the Avoidable
Change the Unacceptable
Accept the Unchangeable

Avoid the Avoidable

The first remedy is to admit that many of the regrets were actually *avoidable*. In most cases, the regretful things that were done by the men and women who responded to our questionnaires were a product of yielding to temptation. For that reason, the individuals were wearing the handcuffs of guilt.

For example, many of the couples voiced sincere remorse for a variety of "sexual indiscretions" (the politically correct jargon for the word *sin*). Some had guilt feelings about living together outside the bonds of marriage. Others regretted their unfaithfulness toward their spouse. Some people had indulged in such things as pornography, and others admitted sexual involvement before marriage that resulted in a pregnancy. Obviously, all of these failures could have been sidestepped by better choices. Yet the sins were committed and the feelings of shame the people feel are very real and debilitating to their marriages. But as devastating as these downfalls may be, there is hope for all spouses who feel "cuffed" by condemnation. That hope is revealed in a song written about one of the saddest stories of regret we have ever heard. First, the story:

> Bill was a youth minister serving at the same church Ann was attending. They became acquainted, fell in love, and became engaged to be married. However, their fairy tale turned into a nightmare.
>
> Before the wedding date arrived, Ann found out she was pregnant. Bill, an up-and-coming-preacher, was convinced that their soon-to-be-obvious moral lapse would likely be the death of his professional career as a minister. He also felt the "situation" would cause a lot of trouble with both his immediate and church families. In desperation, Bill convinced Ann that the only logical solution was for her to have an abortion.
>
> He tried to console her by saying that God would surely understand and would forgive them. He also promised that there could always be more children. Reluctantly, but willing to go along in order to protect their testimony, Ann went to a local clinic and had the "problem" vacuumed from her body.

On the day of their wedding, the young bride slowly made her way down the aisle. She was beautifully attired in her white wedding gown. However, no one could see how she really felt. In tears, Ann relayed the feelings she wrestled with that day. "As I walked down the aisle and everyone was looking at me, smiling, I thought, 'If only these people knew the real me. If they knew what I had done, they wouldn't be smiling at me. Instead, they would throw up.'"

But the congregation of family and friends did smile and gave their approving nods as she walked down to meet her groom, who was wearing a white tuxedo. In her hands she carried a lovely bouquet of flowers, but in her heart she was nearly crushed by the weight of the guilt of innocent blood.

As time went on, Ann carried the guiltiness of that abortion day after day. It wasn't long until the shame began to fester and infect her heart and mind. She became very depressed. She also began to express the loathing and the bitterness she felt toward the husband whom she believed had "made her" get rid of their baby. Not only did she carry her own regrets, but she also became resentful for the pressure she felt from her husband to do something so terrible.

Even after many years of marriage and several other children, her guilt persisted to the point that she finally concluded forgiveness would never come to her. She felt this way because she was convinced that her abortion was a sin so heinous in God's eyes that it out-ranked any other offense. "Even God," she would say, "wouldn't forgive something this bad." Of course, she couldn't have been further from the truth.

There Is Good News

There is a mother, crying tonight
All she can do is grieve
Over and over the question comes
"How could I have been so deceived?"

She feels a wall as she cries to the Lord again
And says, "The Maker of the life I have taken
Will never forgive me this sin."

But I long to tell her
She needs to know
She needs to understand
Her child is not the first life she's taken
There's other blood on her hands.

For the Father in heaven had an innocent Son
Held blameless to the cross
And her sin was among the reasons
That His life was lost.

But there is good news
And she needs to hear it tonight
For the taking of the Savior's life
She is forgiven.

And so it is true
There's no other sin so great
That can't be covered by the grace
Of the Father in heaven.

And so many others are crying tonight
And sadly, they believe
That the love of God came near
But their sin was out of His reach.

But I long to tell them
They need to know
They need to understand
Nothing is worse that they've ever done
Than His blood that's on their hands.

But I long to tell them
They need to know
For the taking of the Savior's life
They are forgiven.

And so it is true
There's no other sin so great
Than can't be covered by the grace
Of the Father in heaven.[1]

In case the story and song about this wife and mother describes your own life, or if it strikes an equally regretful chord in your heart, please consider the comfort in the following verses.

> I, even I, am the one who wipes out your transgressions for My own sake, and I will not remember your sins (Isaiah 43:25).

> If you would direct your heart right and spread out your hand to Him, if iniquity is in your hand, put it far away, and do not let wickedness dwell in your tents; then, indeed, you could lift up your face without moral defect, and you would be steadfast and not fear. For you would forget your trouble, as waters that have passed by, you would remember it. Your life would be brighter than noonday; darkness would be like the morning. Then you would trust, because there is hope; and you would look around and rest securely. You would lie down and none would disturb you, and many would entreat your favor (Job 11:13-19).

Oh, how the pain of avoidable regrets can cause us to shrink back from God and those we love here on the earth. However, as grievous and horrible as our sins may be, they are no match for the boundless love and grace of God, through Christ. Our heavenly Father knows we are weak and pitiful. It is for that reason He sent His sinless Son to buy back our sin-sick souls. When we refuse to accept His pardon and resist forgiving ourselves, even if it is done so out of a sense of personal outrage at our own sin, we literally set ourselves above God. But the truth is, if His righteousness can tolerate and forgive us, then certainly we can, too.

Change the Unacceptable

If you will, take a few moments to look once again at the regrets revealed by the husbands and wives a few pages earlier in this chapter.

As you reread them, make a mental note of how many regrets fall under the category of "changeable." For example, consider the gentleman who didn't finish high school, or the husband who was regretful that he didn't go to college, or the wife who felt her wedding that took place in an outside garden didn't reach to the level of "sacredness" a church sanctuary could have provided.

For these three, we say, "Change the unacceptable!" An earned G.E.D., an online correspondence college course, and a simple, inexpensive vow-renewal ceremony at a home church with friends and family present would remove the regrets!

For the most part, changing the unacceptable requires a little creativity, some manageable financial and time sacrifice, and probably a bit of inconvenience. Still, it surely would be worth it if changing the unacceptable would unlock the restricting "cuffs" that keep us from fully reaching out to our mates.

Steve: I can personally identify with the husband who regretted not finishing college. For me, this has been a nemesis. In 1969, I finished two semesters at Glenville State College in West Virginia. The next year I transferred to Marshall University (home of the Thundering Herd!) where I carried a light load of only 12 hours. It was that year that the military draft lottery was active and my birth date was drawn: #26. Because of my limited class load and not living on campus, the likelihood of obtaining a 4-F deferment for students was questionable. For those reasons, plus I was weary of school and was feeling an adventurous spirit, I ended my college career and headed to the recruiter's office. I joined the U.S. Navy!

I never went back to a campus to complete my post-high school education. Consequently, regret for my decision has nibbled at my sense of confidence for three decades. Finally, I came to grips with the fact that I could change what I considered as unacceptable. Today I am enrolled in a correspondence course. Thanks to the school's kind understanding of folks who have schedules like ours, I will be able to pack three years of college into ten! It will be slow, but I look forward to shedding the regret.

How has this decision affected my marriage? Very simply, if nothing else, by having enrolled in the course and beginning the journey toward a higher education, the gnawing sense of feeling intellectually crippled is going away. In its place is a growing confidence that I will be more able to complement the skills held by my Moody Bible Institute graduate wife. Please understand that never once...never...did she say or do anything that fostered a feeling of inferiority. In fact, she has been my greatest cheerleader. My decision to finish college has been my own struggle. But it's one I can do something about. And if I can do it, you can, too!

Accept the Unchangeable

While changing the unacceptable may be achievable in most cases, to accept the unchangeable is a goal that may require more strength than a person feels they possess. Yet it can be done. Because the events or issues that cannot be altered are often the regrets that seem to do the most damage to a relationship, it is worth the effort to gain resolution. And sometimes, accepting the unchangeable means accepting God's forgiveness.

For example, the sin of premarital sexual involvement can often drive a wedge of distrust between a husband and wife. Sin, in general, never unites but always divides (James 1:14-15). The conflict caused by fornication can kill a couple's ability to find complete emotional and spiritual intimacy later on in their marriage. However, if the couple limits their admissions of transgression to their own relationship, they can face the cause for that division. Then they can accept God's forgiveness of sin—and extend it to each other. The marital joy that can be known in the physical expression of their love can be restored!

All Sin Is Regretful, but Not All Regrets Are Sinful

Even though regrets may not entail sin, the impact can still be just as significant. They must be met with a determination to accept them, to lift our heads, and to courageously continue on together in the journey of marriage.

Again referring to the list of spouse's regrets mentioned earlier, several of their admissions involved non-sin-based decisions that were made earlier in their lives but had serious effects on their relationships. Consider the husband, for instance, who stated, "My wife had to work and leave the children in day care. I know she felt guilty and cheated of time with our kids. It couldn't be helped, though, 'cause I'm disabled. Just because there's a good reason doesn't make it any less disappointing."

Our hearts ache with the remorse this husband must feel. What can he do to overcome the effect of his regret? The answer for him, and anyone who wrestles with these intense feelings, is not necessarily easy. Compassion requires an understanding that to win the battle with the grinding sense of regret and to accept the unchangeable requires an enormous amount of spiritual strength. Thankfully, the power to accept that which cannot be altered is found in God's word.

Philippians 3:13-14 offers some instruction that has a modern, familiar ring to it. The apostle Paul tells us, "...But one thing I *do: forgetting* what lies behind and *reaching* forward to what lies ahead, I *press on* toward the goal for the prize of the upward call of God in Christ Jesus" (emphasis added).

The admonition offered by the ancient writer could be said in these current terms: "Forget it and get on with it." This suggestion could be misconstrued as a simplistic, rude, naive answer to the heart-wrenching, difficult situations that people face. But Paul knew what he was saying. He was well acquainted with the impact regrets can yield.

Before he was encountered by Christ on the road to Damascus as recorded in Acts 9, Paul, who was then called Saul, was a zealous persecutor of Christians. We are first introduced to him in the book of Acts 7:58. During the commission of killing the Christian martyr, Stephen, Saul was right in the middle of the murderous act, lending both his support and his hardy approval to the crime.

After the death of Stephen, a great persecution arose against the church in Jerusalem. Christians were being killed and imprisoned simply because they believed and followed the claims of Christ. The young man leading the mob was none other than Saul of Tarsus. He began to ravage the Christian people. Entering their homes in the middle of the night and dragging away the men and women, he was responsible for leaving children abandoned and sometimes orphaned.

Later, after his conversion to Christ, Paul preached in the very churches that had felt the strap of his passionate fervor of tyranny. The orphans and widows who were by-products of his enthusiastic persecution were among the members of the congregations. As Paul encouraged others to not let their pasts hold them back but to press forward to the future, he indeed was forced to follow his own advice.

Annie: For those of you who face the difficult challenge of accepting the unchangeable, let me, with great compassion and sympathy, encourage you to do what even the apostle Paul *had* to do: forget the past, reach forward, and press on toward the goal. I realize there are some situations that are so painful, so filled with hurts that this must *feel* impossible. However, we must not let our feelings direct our paths and determine our destinies.

Living by our feelings never gets us to where we want to go. For instance, when we eat whatever we *feel* like consuming, we normally end up fat and out of shape. When we buy what we *feel* like buying, we often end up financially broke and needy. When we say what we *feel* like saying, we usually end up friendless and alone. The same principle applies when we allow our feelings to dominate how we think. If we choose to focus on our renegade thoughts, rather than believing the truth of God's word, we sadly end up emotionally paralyzed and "locked up" with regrets.

The admonition of apostle Paul to forget, reach, and press on may provoke some questions: "Can a person actually, by an act of their will, choose to forget? Do individuals really have that much control over what they think about? Isn't forgetting, if it occurs at all, just something that happens over a period of time?" These are reasonable questions to ask. And, once again, in order to find the answers we go to God's word.

One verse that is particularly pertinent to the subject is 2 Corinthians 10:5. We are instructed, once again by Paul, to "...[destroy] speculations and every lofty thing raised up against the knowledge of God, and we are [to take] every thought captive to the obedience of Christ." A person who destroys speculations and anything contrary to what God has said in His word and takes his thoughts captive is a person who is, in essence, stating:

> I choose to see my situation from God's perspective rather than my own. Regardless of how I might think at the moment, I choose to believe and proclaim the immutable truth of God's word over my alterable feelings. As a result of this knowledge, *I will trust that absolutely nothing can touch my life that does not first filter through the loving hands of my merciful, heavenly Father.*

We can face the most difficult circumstances with confidence knowing that the Lord "causes all things to work together for good to those who love God, to those who are called according to His purpose"

(Romans 8:28). A key to unlocking the chains of "unchangeable regrets" is found in agreeing with God that regardless of how horrible the situation might be, God is in control. He has declared to those who love Him and desire His purpose in their life, that He will cause all things to work to further that plan. Even though it may be painful, ultimately there is no other way to find peace in the midst of the unchangeable.

Annie: There was a time in my life when I considered the advice to "forget and get over" the hurts generated by the past not only insensitive, but utterly impossible. My mind was tormented by hurtful memories and painful remembrances of a childhood sexual assault by a stranger. My thoughts kept me imprisoned by my past. I was filled with bitterness, anger, and a relentless feeling of regret. I experienced a sense of mourning over being robbed of everything good and innocent. I continued to live in dread and remorse until I began to recognize a life-altering truth. Everything changed when I finally realized that the Lord was bigger and stronger than my tortured mind.

As I began to diligently study God's word, He began to set me free. Using passages such as Jeremiah 29:11-13, He changed my focus from hurts and disappointments of the past to a vision and a desire to reach forward toward the future: "'For I know the plans that I have for you,' declares the Lord, 'plans for welfare and not for calamity to give you a future and a hope. Then you will call upon Me and come and pray to Me, and I will listen to you. And you will seek Me and find Me when you search for Me with all your heart.'" Based on God's comforting promise to pave the road ahead with His glorious hope, I can personally assure you that it's not enough to just let go of the past. We must take the next step and reach forward to His future for us. It is the only path to the fullness of joy, especially for husbands and wives.

Steve: I have been married to Annie for many years, and I am deeply aware of her earlier journey from regretful rage to becoming the sweetest woman I know. For that reason, to all who face the momentous task of accepting the unchangeable, I can confidently confirm that Paul's instructions that Annie followed are both wise and effective. In fact, I have been the main benefactor of her courage to "take every thought captive to the obedience of Christ." Her willingness to allow God's work to alter her thinking has been a valuable blessing to our marriage. Because of that, I urge you to consider her example.

For those whose quest to accept the unchangeable may not include such excruciating challenges as Annie's, I add the following suggestion. Many years ago I heard a Bible teacher address the struggle to accept things in our lives that we cannot change. His admonition was to "put new meanings on old problems." To say it another way, "Eat the chicken and leave the bone."

To illustrate this exercise of the heart and how it can yield an inner peace in regard to our inability to change certain parts of the past, I offer the following lyric. It is a story about a man who had a dream since his youth to be a hunting guide in the big western states of our country. The story is told from his son's point of view.

The Guide

His high-school classroom felt like prison walls
When November came
It's hard to hear your teacher talk
When a deer stand calls your name.

At night he'd read his Field & Stream
It was back in 1962
The stories and the pictures fed a young hunter's dream
He knew exactly what he wanted to do.

He said, "Someday I'm gonna go out West
Where the mountains kiss the sky
I'll make a name, I'm gonna be the best
They'll come to me
I'm gonna be a huntin' guide!"

He said, "If I can just make it till next spring
I'll wear that cap and gown
Then I'll go out and climb up in those Rockies
And maybe never come back down!"

But in September of his senior year
Something woke him from his dream
He said he'd never seen a finer deer
Her name was Mary Jean.

And it was on that day his western plans
They began to drift back east
Strange how love can change a man
Guess it can tame even the wildest beast.

Well, thirty seasons have come and gone
He still loves my mother, Mary Jean
But as we hunt together on this November dawn
He talks again about that dream.

I see regret in his eyes like that morning mist
That paints the wheat field gray
But when my shot connects in the distance
His sadness goes away.

And he says, "O, I think you got 'im, son
Wish you could see your face
Strange how we can feel so close
In such a wide open space."

So I said, "Dad, remember when I was younger
I went out searching for the truth?
And for a while I wandered on over
To the dark side of my youth.

"But I couldn't forget how I felt so safe with you
In the woods by your side
You're the reason I came back home, you led me to the trophy of Grace
You were my soul's huntin' guide!

"So, Dad, I'm glad you didn't go out west
Where the mountains kiss the sky
I would've never known you are the best
And I thank you for being my huntin' guide
You're leading me to heaven, Dad
And I thank you for being my huntin' guide."[2]

The son in this story was able to assist his dad in facing the regrets and finding the good in the unchangeable. He did so by helping his father see how a decision made long ago made a positive, spiritual effect on the future of the generations that would follow him. Perhaps, by taking the time to ponder the truth that God can be trusted to "order our steps" (see Psalm 37:23), some husbands and wives can find peace in knowing that He really does cause all things to work together for our good, as well as the good of those we love.

No Regrets

Regrets seem to come in degrees. Some are not as difficult to deal with as others. To whatever extent you as a husband or wife may be confronting regrets, we hope your goal will be set as high as the one inspired in us by our friend, Jim. Here's his story.

Steve: Unlike my father, who has become a compassionate master at knowing what to say to others in times of grief, I do not do as well. My "gold mine of wisdom nuggets" seems to often shut down in the face of intense sadness. For that reason, I did not look forward to our planned rendezvous with Jim in his hometown.

Only a few weeks earlier he had said goodbye to his 33-year-old wife, Donna. She was a victim of a rare form of lung cancer. Jim and his three young children were left to mourn the passing of this sweet wife and mother. *What will I say to Jim?* I wondered as we drove into his state.

As is so often the case, those who grieve are, by need, drawn closer to God's grace and strength. As a result, when we met with him, Jim was not as comforted by my words as I was inspired by his. During our restaurant meal he told us something that, to this day, has echoed in the ears of my heart more often than nearly any other words another husband/father has said to me through the years. In reference to his relationship with Donna, Jim said with a reserved smile, "I have no regrets."

Morally, physically, emotionally, and spiritually Jim had accomplished a mission that many husbands and wives dream of doing. Though he had told his wife "goodbye," in his heart of hearts he was confident that no wedges existed between them. While there were certainly tears that ran like a river at Donna's passing, there were no floods of sorrow for unkind ways he had treated her, for unresolved conflicts, for "word-wounds" that were left unhealed, or remorse for not being more of a helper with the kids. He had done all he could do, and we could see in his eyes that his spirit was at rest.

As Annie and I left the restaurant that day and drove away, I prayed silently that if ever I sat on his side of the table, my admission could be the same as Jim's. A few days later, I wrote the following lyric to honor my friend's worthy accomplishment. I did so in hopes that his story would inspire other spouses as it encouraged me.

No Regrets

He's got a lonely heart,
He's got an empty room,
He's got an empty bed....
It happened much too soon.
He's got some memories
He will never forget
But one thing he doesn't have—
He has no regrets.

He remembers the day
About a year ago
When they told her the news—
He held her close
And in the time she had remaining
He didn't know
How much she'd be changing.

'Cause, his love that was strong
Through all those years,
Had to be even stronger
To hold back the tears,
When her angry words,
Would cut him so deeply
But somehow he knew
It was pain that was speaking.

And the girl that he married
Had a spark in her eyes
That won a young boy's heart
Kept a man's love alive.
And when the thief stole that spark
And his nights grew colder,

He didn't seek other fires—
He was warmed just to hold her.

And he remembers the night
She called out his name.
He held her hand
'Til the morning came.
And in the still of the night
She told him goodbye—
He'll be glad he was with her
For the rest of his life.

But now, he's got a lonely heart
He's got an empty room,
He's got an empty bed....
It happened much too soon.
He's got some memories
He will never forget
But one thing he doesn't have—
He has no regrets.[3]

ten

Vintage Wine or Vinegar?

*A*nnie: The Chapman household experienced an interesting phenomenon a few years ago. Within an 11-month period of time we gained a son-in-law and a daughter-in-law. For weeks upon end we were up to our eyebrows in wedding paraphernalia. On every table in the house you could find magazines containing articles on how to plan the perfect wedding. There were periodicals the size of encyclopedias displaying incredibly beautiful wedding gowns and attire. And, of course, there was an assortment of pamphlets disclosing where to go on (but not how to pay for) a fantasy honeymoon.

One day, in the midst of all the plotting and planning for the weddings, the two young brides and their young men were standing in our kitchen. The grooms-to-be had each purchased a bouquet of beautiful flowers for their young ladies. As the girls stood looking admirably at the sprays of color, while casting loving glances toward their fellows, one of the brides-to-be said, "Isn't young love wonderful?"

I started to respond with my full agreement that love, at any stage, is a beautiful mystery. However, an overwhelming thought suddenly passed through my head and heart, and I couldn't resist saying it out loud. "Oh, yes, young love is wonderful, but there ain't nothin' like *old* love!"

Steve was standing nearby when our little female exchange took place, and when he heard my answer he looked at me, sipped his coffee, and quietly grinned from ear to ear. Within 20 minutes he had written the following lyric.

Old Love

Young love can be like a runaway train
You've got sparks on the rails, but the engine has no flame
And when it comes to the hills, it just can't make the climb
Baby, I like what we've got; it keeps on rolling through time

'Cause we've got,
Old love, steady and true
Don't have to go fast
When you know how to move
After all these years we just know what to do
We've got old love, steady and true.

Now, don't you feel sorry
For all the young lovers
Got to wait a long time, before they discover

Old love, steady and true
Don't have to go fast
When you know how to move
After all these years we just know what to do
We've got, old love, steady and true.[1]

Steve: My attempt to put a lyrical exclamation point on my wife's very stimulating statement about "mature love" eventually became a song that has struck a happy chord in a lot of ears. We thoroughly enjoy watching older couples smile and gently elbow each other when we perform the "Old Love" tune. Their jovial responses tell us that we're not alone in having discovered the joy of longevity.

Like a Fine Wine

Listening to our children's prewedding talk about their plans for a life together, we couldn't help but reflect on the strong, boundless energy of young love. However, as tremendous as youthful passion might be, we are compelled to admit that old love is a thousand times more potent.

A very wise woman once said, "Young love, the raging river, makes of the later years a mighty deep and plentiful ocean!" (Thank you, Annie, for your wisdom!)

But as powerful as young love can be, it does have a certain fragility that must not be overlooked. Consider this analogy: Wine, as it is allowed to age, increases in value and sweetness *if* it is protected and attended. Sadly enough however, wine, when it is ignored and mistreated, can turn sour and bitter. And like a delicate, fine wine, love must also receive careful attention through the years. For instance, when wine is exposed to impurities and the environment where it is stored becomes hostile to the product, then it not only loses its value and intended use, it actually becomes nothing more than worthless vinegar.

Passing the Sweet Cup

In light of the picture of a sweetly seasoned relationship that a well-aged wine can provide, those of us who are in our "old love" stage of married life must realize that we have a tremendous responsibility. There are generations of young ones looking to see how it's done. They want to see that a couple *can* be married "till death do they part" and still be happy and even care about each other. All around them in the tabloids and movie magazines they see couples proclaiming their undying love. There are full-color layouts of the wonderful lives the celebrities share, as well as their elaborate and expensive weddings. Then, by the next edition it seems, they are announcing their divorce because "they have grown apart."

It's up to us, the parents and grandparents, to lead the way, to pass a cup of sweetness on to the young ones. We have the potential to show them that love truly can survive. Not only can a couple stay together, but they can remain faithful, loving, and happy. The wine of romance really does get better and sweeter with time.

Unfortunately, too many seasoned husbands and wives are passing a cup of spirits to the younger ones that has become rancid to everyone's taste. There's hardly anything more bitter than an older couple who has let their love turn to vinegar. Unfortunately, it's usually their children and grandchildren who get to listen to the old folks snip and snap and throw verbal darts at one another. These marrieds need a miracle—one that would be just as amazing as the water-into-wine kind. They need their sour-vinegar attitudes turned back into the sweet wine of caring

love. Whether either of them wants to admit it or not, what these husbands and wives should be telling each other as their loves matures, is:

> "After these many years of being married to you, I want to
> know the best is yet to come. I want us to fully enjoy
> every minute we have left together. I want our relationship
> to deepen and grow sweeter. I am willing to do whatever
> it takes to enrich our lives together until we get to that "old
> love" era. And maybe, by being a couple whose marriage
> is sweet to the taste of our children, they, too, will want
> what we have."

Wisdom from Others

As a way to offer some insight on how to correctly tend to the wine
of love, we have enlisted the wisdom of other older couples who were
kind enough to respond to some very probing questions. The target
group consisted of people who had been married at least 20 years.
Hopefully, their perspectives will provide encouragement and serve as
some helpful instruction to all young lovers.

Question 1: Looking back on your early years of marriage, what
seemed so important at the time but now doesn't seem like such a big
deal?

* We were really concerned with how great we looked, how
  much money we had, and what everyone thought about us.
  (Husband of 30 years)

* We fought a lot about the division of household chores. We
  wasted a lot of time on insignificant stuff like that. (Wife of 22
  years)

* Financial success was one of our main goals. We spent a lot of
  time acquiring possessions. It all seems so shallow now. (Wife
  of 30 years)

* Work was my number-one priority. My work week was
  between 60 to 70 hours on the average. By the time the
  weekend came around, I was so tired I couldn't do anything
  else. I wish I would have spent more time with my family.
  (Husband of 40 years)

- I spent a lot of time thinking about what other people thought of me. (Wife of 25 years)

- Having a clean house consumed much of my time and thinking. I guess I thought the way our house looked reflected on me as a person. I wasn't a very nice wife or mother since I was always nagging, trying to keep everything perfect. (Wife of 21 years)

- Most of my emotional energy went into pleasing my husband. I felt like I had to keep him happy, no matter what that cost me personally. I gave up my own sense of self in order to make him feel important. (Wife of 47 years)

- Sex was always an issue in our marriage. I wanted it more frequently than my wife. We fought about it weekly. (Husband of 25 years)

- I felt like I had to be the perfect wife and mother. I spent all my time trying to fulfill an impossible task and achieve what I've now determined to be a fantasy. (Wife of 33 years)

Sex, money, possessions, and how others looked at them were the reoccurring comments of both husbands and wives.

Question 2. What advice would you offer to young couples getting married today?

- Make sure you really know one another.

- Be sure you have the blessing of your parents and your church leaders.

- Make sure you get counseling for your own personal issues. Your problems should be resolved before you take on someone else's problems. Marriage is easier if you don't bring a lot of your junk into it.

- Talk about important subjects such as finances, raising children, and spiritual beliefs. When they're young, couples tend to believe that love conquers all. Unfortunately, that's not true. You need a whole lot more than chemistry to make it through the tough times. A couple needs to have some basic points of agreement.

* Be right with God. Unless that relationship is online, nothing else will work.

* Remember, no decision is unimportant. Talk to one another about decisions, both major and minor ones.

* Make sure the person you're marrying is someone you can respect. Looking good, feeling good, having a great personality—none of those things matter if the person you're marrying is a nasty, dishonest person of low character. Keep your eyes open before your marriage.

* Don't get married too soon. When you're young, you don't have a sense of who you are yet. Know who you are before you try to merge with someone else.

* Go to premarital class and learn how to communicate with one another.

* Be careful about the amount of debt you bring into a marriage. Each individual should try to clean up their own financial situation before the wedding. It is a built-in conflict when you get married broke. The spouse who didn't have the debt will begin to resent the pressure the other one brings into the marriage.

* I recommend going to a financial/budgeting class to learn how to deal with money.

* Don't get involved sexually while you're dating. When you are focused on the physical, time that should be used talking and learning about each other is squandered away doing things you ought not to be doing. A sexually based dating relationship is actually very shallow.

* Center on the three "C's": Christ, commitment, and communication.

* Marriage is forever. A young couple should get married knowing that divorce is not an option. With that in mind, you should be very careful who you marry. Only marry someone you are willing to be with until you die.

- Put Christ at the center of your marriage. Let Him be the one you seek to please. Jesus is to be the winner of every fight, and the reason to make up when you're angry.

- Before you marry your mate, ask yourself this question: "Would I choose this person to be my trusted friend?" Any answer other than a resounding, "Yes!" is reason to run...and run fast. It's not enough to "love" your spouse, you need to "like" him or her also.

Question 3: What do you dread most about growing older?

- Loss of health.

- The death of my spouse.

- Physical limitations.

- Fear of the uncertain.

- Not finishing strong.

- Being a burden to my children, both physically and financially.

- Alzheimer's disease.

- Financial ruin.

- Some are afraid of dying; I'm afraid of living.

- I dread not leaving a good legacy for my grandchildren.

- I fear losing my mind and not being able to find it.

- I'm afraid I will never love my wife the way she wanted. I would die a failure.

- Living in an ever-increasing liberal world where God is dishonored.

- Seeing how my grandchildren turn out.

- That my husband will die without Christ.

- Physical pain.

Steve: Allow me to interrupt if you will. The "physical pain" issue is something I dread as well. I'm frankly tired of all the "senior citizen" jokes I have to deal with now that my head has become a shingleless roof. Where's the end to the cruelty? I propose being helpful to one another in this brittle time of our lives. For that reason, I want to lead the way by telling you about a new exercise program for those of us over 50 who want to build up our shoulder and arm muscles. This will be especially useful to all bowhunters. Here it is…start with a 5-pound potato bag in each hand. Hold it out at arm's length parallel to the floor for one full minute. Repeat daily for two weeks. Then go to 10-pound potato bags and do the same. Work your way up to 50-pound and then 100-pound potato bags. When you can finally hold them out at arm's length for one full minute every day, then add potatoes! But be careful when you get to this level.

Question 4: What is something you and your spouse have done that has kept your marriage sweet and satisfying?

- Focus on each other.

- Going places together.

- Tried to put my spouse's need before my own.

- Communicate and spend time together.

- Annual family vacations.

- We go to married renewal retreats.

- We work together. For example, he helps with the dishes, I help haul firewood.

- At night, before we go to sleep, we try to read a little bit out of a marriage devotional book.

- We kept a regular date night. We let nothing interfere with it.

- We like to go out for lunch since my husband is retired. It's cheaper than dinner, and we don't like to be out late.

- We care about each other's mental outlook. We try to keep life as stress-free for each other as we can.

- We go away at least three times a year, together of course—just the two of us.

- Hold hands when we're driving, or when we're drifting off to sleep. Physical affection is very important.

- I ask my husband every day, "What can I do for you today that will make your life more enjoyable?" Then I try to do it.

- Keeping Christ at the center of our lives and marriage keeps it better.

- We have been honoring and kind to our parents. I think God has blessed us for that effort with a loving, sweet marriage.

- We maintain our friendship with one another. We do fun things together.

- We talk kindly to one another. We are polite and courteous to each other.

Annie: Of all the comments in response to this question, two are worth special attention. One is the saddest the other is the most profound.

- We do nothing to help our marriage. That's why it isn't sweet or satisfying.

- We realize the success of our marriage affects a lot more people than just the two of us. We have a responsibility to generations that come after us to make this relationship not only work but be a glowing example to our children and grandchildren.

Question 5: What challenges do you think young couples face today that you didn't have to deal with 20 years ago?

- Competition for time. There are so many things to pull a couple away from the marriage.

- There's much more pressure on young couples to have a lot of stuff. When we got married, credit card debt was not an issue. Now, every television advertisement, every magazine or movie tells these young kids they need and deserve whatever they see. I feel sorry for them.

* The hectic, stressful pace on young families is incredible. Everyone in the family has a full schedule of events and meetings. There's no time to just sit down together and talk and find out what's going on in the family. Unfortunately, sometimes the only way young parents know what's happening with their children is when the kids get in trouble.

* Young families don't have the job security my generation enjoyed. If a person worked hard for a company and was loyal to the cause, they could count on staying all the way through and retiring comfortably. Now, with corporate take-overs, downsizing, and businesses going bankrupt, there's no guarantee of a job or the investment of all the years of a person's life. This causes a lot of fear and anxiety in a marriage.

* I fear the moral decline of our society and nation. I'm afraid that my grandchildren will grow up in a completely different world than me or my children. Young families face problems with computer porn, Internet threats to our children, drugs, and sexual materials in entertainment and schools. It's so scary; sometimes I wonder if our world is going to survive.

* Of course, my generation never even thought about terrorists, school shootings, or drive-by murders. This is a violent world.

* There's a lot of pressure on young couples to be highly educated. It seems like a person can't really get a good, high-paying job without the advanced degrees. Of course, that means going into debt for school. These young couples start out sometimes tens of thousands of dollars in debt. Is it any wonder they feel financially defeated from the beginning?

* Families never seem to be able to eat dinner together any more. They plan too many things that keep them separated from one another.

* There are a lot of opportunities as well as temptations to be unfaithful to one another. When I was a young wife, I stayed home with the children. Most of the time I couldn't have

gotten into mischief if I had wanted to. Nowadays, both husbands and wives are out of the home supporting a lifestyle that requires two incomes. They are working away from each other all day, laboring side by side with other attractive, well-dressed people of the opposite sex. Then they come home at the end of a long, difficult day; they are exhausted and their emotional bank is empty. Month after month and year after year of this pattern, and the couples are primed for marital disaster.

The gems of wisdom in these honest answers are worth pondering, especially for the younger couples. As you do, may those who have gone before you help direct, or redirect, you in your desire to make it together to the end of your journey. And finally, may the tale that time has written about you as a couple be as powerfully inspiring as the true story a Georgia grandson told us about his grandparents. Here's a parting lyric about two people who definitely achieved the priceless crown of old love.

Let Me Take Her Home

We thought it would be best
To put our Grandma in that home
But Grandpa's heart was broken
It left him all alone.
But we didn't think him able
In the winter of his years
To give her the help she needed
But he said through his tears,

"Let me take her home with me
'Cause I made a promise I have to keep
And I know that's where she'd rather be
Let me take her home
I can't leave her here alone
Let me take her home with me."

Every day he made the journey
To see the one who wore his name
And he'd sit with her for hours

She never knew he came.
He was her faithful friend
Till the close of every day
Then he would beg for mercy
As they would send him away
And he'd say

"Let me take her home with me
'Cause I made a promise
I have to keep
And I know that's where she would rather be
Let me take her home
I can't leave her here alone
Let me take her home with me."

Then one night it happened
Grandpa went home early
At least that's what the nurses assumed
But he was hiding in a closet
And when the lights went out
Quietly he slipped into her room
Then with all his strength remaining
He gathered her in his arms
His one and only love of sixty years
And down the darkened hallway
To the safety of his Buick
He carried her
And whispered in her ear...
"I'm gonna take you home with me

'Cause I made a promise I have to keep
And I know that's where you would rather be
I'm gonna take you home
I can't leave you here alone
I'm gonna take you home with me."

Well, he proved that love was able
'Cause he was with her till the end
And before the year was over
We said "goodbye" to him
And now they both are resting

On a hill outside of town
But in the hearts of all who knew him
These words are written down...

"Let me take her home with me."[2]

"The memory of the righteous is blessed."
Proverbs 10:7

A Talkative
Quiet Time for Couples

❧ ❧ ❧

Questions and Comments for Discussion

The Meat-Loaf Revelation

"When wishing won't work."

Annie: Wouldn't it be wonderful if all we had to do was read a book and all of our problems would be solved? I've tried this technique. For instance, when I needed to lose some excess weight, I purchased diet books, read the success stories, bought the expensive exercise equipment, and earnestly prayed asking God to somehow superimpose His will and strength into me to accomplish my goal. Even with the best of intentions and the most sincere of motives, it wasn't until I was willing to take a painful look at myself that I became willing to do the hard work. I began to slowly see a change in my body shape only when I started saying yes to right choices and no to the ones that thwarted my plan.

The same is true when it comes to developing and strengthening our relationship with our spouses. No amount of hopeful thinking or noble intent will bring about the intimate and loving relationship we desire. Only when we are willing to do the hard work of talking and listening to one another will we come to know the hearts of our beloveds.

We shared our story of the "meat loaf" revelation in the opening pages of this book. We said, "There comes a time in the relationship between a husband and wife when it's time to stop being miserable, stop complaining, and start telling the other what we want."

Before the two of you, as husband and wife, start to tell each other what may become your "meat loaf" revelation, take a moment to ask God to open your hearts and minds to one another. Then with your Bibles, sit down together and read some passages concerning how to speak your mind in truth *and* in love. As you read these verses, keep in mind this is not the time for one spouse to teach and the other to listen. Take turns sharing what each passage means to you.

Read 1 Peter 3:8-12.

Now, thoughtfully, write down three things you need to do that will help bring a sense of peace and encouragement to your mate.

1.

2.

3.

Chapter One

Prepared, Repaired, Paired

What husbands and wives aren't telling each other…in the beginning of their marriage:

> *"I want to meet your deepest needs and be your dreammate, but as a weak human being I cannot do it. I know very well that is a God-sized job. I am quite aware, however, that even though I don't have the power to make you happy, I can make your life miserable and even be a hindrance to God's work of peace in your heart. As much as I would like to help you, only He can make your spirit smile forever."*

God Prepares Us

Everyone has a love story to tell. We gladly shared our account of meeting in middle school and then developing a friendship through our high school years. Even though we had been acquainted with one another and shared similar interest, we didn't really know each other.

My grandmother said concerning the whole dating scene, "You don't really get to know one another in a courting situation. In reality, you just as well run into a crowd, grab a stranger's hand, and marry him. That's how well you know your spouse when you get hitched." There may be a lot of truth to grandma's philosophy; however, I don't recommend it for any future brides and grooms. The point should be well taken, though.

We go into our marriages with great expectations and even greater promises. A young groom, in all sincerity, may promise his bride that he will never disappoint her. With his heart and words, he vows that she will always feel loved, secure, valued, and cozy. Oh, what a sweet assurance! Too bad he is incapable of keeping such a pledge.

In the same way, a young bride brings her beauty, youth, and vitality to a marriage. Being on her best behavior, as they both are, she graces his life with a lovely appearance, kind words, a sweet disposition, and amiable countenance. Her unspoken promise is to support him in anything and everything he wants to do. Her pledge of undying cooperation and love are also vows she is incapable of delivering on.

1. Read together Romans 8:28. How does this apply to your marriage?

2. Keeping in mind that God has been preparing you as individuals, share with your spouse a specific time when you have sensed God's work in your life.

3. What difficult situation, as described in Romans 8:28, did He "work for good" on your behalf?

God Repairs Us

As much as we might wish, we cannot make one another "happy." Only God can fix the broken places in our lives and fill them with His peace and forgiveness. Even though we cannot repair the shattered places in our spouses, we can help create an atmosphere in our marriages where our beloveds can more easily hear and respond to God's reconstructive work in their hearts.

1. Read together Romans 5:1-9.

2. Take turns sharing with one another how God demonstrated His great mercy toward you by providing the payment for your sins through the finished work of Jesus Christ on the cross.

3. Share with one another when you came to know and accept Christ as your Savior. Never underestimate the power in giving your testimony. Revelation 12:11 says, "And they overcame him [Satan] because of the blood of the Lamb and because of the *word of their testimony*, and they did not love their life even when faced with death" (emphasis added).

As the husbands and wives who answered the questionnaire revealed, we bring into our marriages a boatload of hurts, painful experiences, and unfulfilled expectations.

4. After reading Romans 5:3-4, write down some of the emotions you struggle with.

As a wife, the one emotion I struggle with the most is…

As a husband, the one emotion I struggle with the most is…

5. As a wife, I believe the root of that woundedness originated from…

As a husband, I believe the root of that woundedness originated from…

6. This struggle affects my relationship with my mate in the following ways…

7. One thing my spouse could do to help me in this area would be…

God Pairs Us

1. Read together 1 Corinthians 3:11 and Matthew 7:24.

2. Discuss how the firm foundation of Christ has kept your home together. Recount the storms that have assailed your family, and give God the praise for His help.

3. Together say a prayer of confession. Confess any moral failure, any sexual sin, sensual manipulation, or defrauding that went on between the two of you prior to your wedding.

4. Pray a prayer of thanksgiving for God's preparation in your lives when you were singles.

5. Give praise and thanks to God for the reparative work He is doing in your hearts and relationship.

6. Ask God, once again, to be the firm foundation that will allow your marriage to survive whatever may be ahead.

Chapter Two

I Need a Teammate, Not a Cell Mate

What husbands and wives aren't telling each other…about working together as a team:

> *"I know that in order for our marriage to be a success, we need to work at it together. But it's hard to feel like your teammate when there are times you make me feel more like a cell mate. To sing "I need you" is not so easy when I feel hopelessly locked behind the bars of matrimony."*

"Marriage is a wonderful institution. If it weren't for marriage, husbands and wives would have to fight with perfect strangers." Obviously this comment has a rather jaded ring to it. The first thing wrong with this statement is that husbands and wives don't have to fight—at least not in a hurtful, hateful way. And second, the stranger only seems perfect.

1. What does your spouse do or say that makes you feel miserable?

2. What does your spouse do or say that makes you feel happy?

3. Read some of the responses given by husbands and wives on pages 22-23, 27-29. Do any of these answers sound familiar? Let the honesty of their replies serve as a catalyst for your own conversation.

4. Give each other the freedom to lovingly express some feelings that may have been hidden for quite a while. Remember, you can only feel like a teammate, rather than a cell mate, when you do the hard work of talking *and* listening.

Some husbands and wives have resigned themselves to the idea that marriage is an institution, and they feel like they've received a life sentence. If this is how you or your spouse feels, it's time to talk to one another. God has a much better plan in mind for the two of you as a team.

Read Ecclesiastes 4:9-12

1. Have the two of you found a way to work together that produces a good return for your effort (verse 9)?

2. In what area of your marriage, do you recognize the need to work together?

With the children?

Around the house?

Doing a hobby?

3. In what ways have you lifted up your mate when he or she fell down under the pressure of circumstances (verse 10)?

4. What did it mean to you to have the support of your spouse during a difficult time?

5. How did it make you feel when your spouse "let you down"? Can you forgive your mate when he or she fails to "be there" for you?

6. What can you learn from these passages?

Matthew 6:14-15—

Matthew 18:2-6—

Ephesians 4:32—

Colossians 3:12-14—

7. In what ways have you made your marriage a warm and safe place for your spouse (Ecclesiastes 4:11)?

8. List some little ways you have shown love toward your spouse. (*It looks like dishes, but it feels like love; it looks like a turkey hunt, but it feels like love.*)

   •

   •

   •

9. Tell each other what looks and feels like love to you. Be truthful, but at the same time be kind and loving.

10. What changes can the two of you make, starting today, that will make your marriage look like the wagon wheel described on page 24? (See Ecclesiastes 4:12.)

11. What is the biggest obstacle that hinders you from fully teaming together and pursuing a Christ-centered home?

12. What can you do to overcome that problem?

Chapter Three

A Partner, Not a Parent

What husbands and wives aren't telling each other…about how they need to be treated:

> *"I need you to be my partner, not my parent. I feel suffocated and frustrated when you treat me like a child and boss me around. We can never truly love one another the way we need to until you are willing to treat me like an adult."*

Nearly 50 percent of all husbands and wives we surveyed cited "feeling controlled" by their spouses as a significant problem. The responses given by the husbands and wives to the question "Is your spouse a controlling person?" reveal that the tendency to control is not a gender issue—it's a sin issue.

1. Read together the responses given by husbands and wives on pages 38-42. If you identify with any of the answers, put a star by it. With humility of heart, discuss each of the scenarios flagged.

2. Take turns discussing why the answers resonate with you. Also describe how the issues mentioned make you feel. Jot down some of the feelings expressed by your mate.

Men and women are equally hurt and feel devalued when their spouses disregard their opinions and consider their wishes unimportant.

It is said, "The road to ruin is kept in good repair." Couples who are intent on "ruling over the other" are on the road to ruining their marriage; however, it doesn't have to be that way.

3. Spend some time reading 1 Corinthians 13. Take special notice of verses 1 through 5.

4. How do you measure up to the definition of what love is and isn't?

5. First Corinthians 13:4 says love is patient. The word *patient* literally means to feel "long-tempered" with people (as opposed to short-tempered). Chrysostom, an early church father, said, "It is a word which is used of the man who is wronged and who has it in his power to avenge himself but will never do it."[1]

In what way have you shown your spouse *patient love?*

6. Read Romans 15:5. Ask God in prayer to give you the power to act accordingly.

7. Love is kind (1 Corinthians 13:4). The word *kind* literally means to *act* in a beneficial way. To be kind is the counterpart to being patient. Being kind is not just a feeling; it is an action. *Kind* means not only feeling generous, but also acting on those feelings by giving. It means desiring the best for someone else's welfare and actively working toward it.[2]

Realizing that kindness is an action, read Luke 6:35-38 and Ephesians 4:32. Talk about how you can apply these scriptures to your marriage.

8. Love is not jealous (1 Corinthians 13:4). Love and jealousy cannot live together; they are mutually exclusive. There are two kinds of jealousy. One kind says, "I want what someone else has." The other kind says, "I wish they didn't have what they have."

If there is jealousy in your marriage, ask God to help you rid yourself of that plague.[3]

9. Read together James 3:14-16 and Proverbs 27:4. What do these verses say to you?

10. Love does not brag (1 Corinthians 13:4). The word *brag* is not used anywhere else in the New Testament. It literally means to "talk conceitedly." Bragging is the flip side of jealousy. Jealousy is wanting what someone else has; bragging is trying to make someone want what you have. Both are destructive to a marriage. Bragging puts ourselves first and is the epitome of pride.[4]

Read Philippians 2:6-8. How would your marriage improve if you lived by this passage?

11. First Corinthians 13:4 says love is not arrogant. There is no room left in pride for love. Proverbs 8:13 says, "Pride and arrogance and the evil way and the perverted mouth, I hate." And Proverbs 16:18 warns us, "Pride goes before destruction, and a haughty spirit before stumbling."

Are there areas where pride has harmed your marriage? If yes, confess these areas to the Lord. Pray with your spouse that love will win in your marriage and that pride will be cast out.

12. Love does not act unbecomingly (1 Corinthians 13:5). Love is not rude. A controlling person is an extremely rude one. Unhealthy control over others is achieved by violating everything love is. When you care about a person, you treat them with courtesy and manners.

List two ways you can be more considerate of each other's feelings.

a.

b.

13. Love does not seek its own (1 Corinthians 13:5). Love is not selfish. If you want to know the number-one problem in your marriage, go look in the mirror. (And while you're looking at yourself, be assured we'll be searching out a mirror to see the primary problems in our marriage.) Self. It can all be boiled down to...self.

Discuss ways the two of you can show selfless love to each other. Take turns expressing needs that, perhaps, have gone unrequested until now.

14. There may be no greater scriptural help for the married couple than the truth found in Matthew 20:26-28. Read these verses together.

15. Make a list of three things each of you can do that will demonstrate your desire to serve one another.

Husband

a.

b.

c.

Wife

a.

b.

c.

16. First Corinthians 13:5 says love is not provoked. Love is not easily angered. The kind of anger indicated is "convulsive or sudden outburst of emotion or action." True love is not easily shaken by others' actions or circumstances. Anger itself is not a sin.

Read Matthew 21:12-14. What happens in verse 14?

17. List the last few times you remember being angry. What provoked your reaction?

18. Love does not take into account wrongs suffered—love doesn't hold a grudge (1 Corinthians 13:5). The word for "taking account" is a bookkeeping term. It indicates keeping a permanent record of "foul ups." It doesn't feel like love when a spouse keeps throwing mistakes and blunders in one's face. What do these passages say to you?

Romans 4:8—

2 Corinthians 5:19—

Matthew 18:21-35—

Psalm 103:12—

Chapter Four

The Challenge of Change

What husbands and wives aren't telling each other about the inevitable changes that are a part of marriage:

> *"I know we may have different expectations when it comes to change, but I must say, since we got married you've changed in some ways I didn't expect and you haven't changed in the ways I expected."*

From the beginning husbands and wives are set up for conflict and disappointment. Men are a lot like God in that men are the same yesterday, today, and forever. (A little divine humor.) Men marry women hoping they stay the same. They want their wives, some 30 years later to be exactly the way they were the day they got married. They want the women to have the same hairdo, the same waist size, and wear the same pair of black shoes.

Women, on the other hand, marry men with the hope and the expectation of changing them as soon as possible. So change is a central theme. Men resisting it, and women insisting on it. The only hope for couples to live in harmony when it comes to these major differences is to be bendable. Without flexibility, the family tree is apt to break.

With limited time and focus we have chosen to address what many of the husbands and wives wanted to talk about. The change that impacted them the most as a couple was the challenge of having children around.

Now would be a good time to take a second look at the comments made by the fathers on our questionnaire. They answered the question, "How has having children changed your relationship with your spouse?" Their comments will provide some good discussion material for you. (See pages 52-54.)

1. In what ways have you tried to keep your marital relationship your focus, while fulfilling the demands of carrying for your children?

2. List three specific things you can do or have been doing, as a couple, that would serve to strengthen your relationship.

   •

   •

   •

3. Are there any special challenges with your children, small or grown, that have been particularly difficult to handle? Express to your spouse how much you appreciated his or her help during that time. Be specific.

   Or share how it made you feel when you perceived you were carrying the load all by yourself.

4. Is there an area of parenting that exposes your differing views and varied values as they concern your children? Discuss calmly some common ground you might find to help alleviate this dilemma.

5. Read Psalm 127. Pray for God's help as you both serve together as watchmen over your family. Stop and pray together, committing each one of your children to the Lord. Ask for divine wisdom on how to keep your marriage your central focus, even as you raise your children.

Chapter Five

Connected or Co-Naked

What husbands and wives aren't telling each other in the area of physical intimacy:

> *"Somehow, we've got to find a bridge between the wife's need to be connected and the husband's need to be co-naked. As a wife, I need you to be willing to be emotionally naked before me, so that I can feel connected to you. As a husband, I need you to be willing to be physically naked before me, and meet my sexual needs, in order for me to feel connected to you."*

We've heard this said many times: "When a couple's sexual relationship is good, it's only 10 percent important. But when there's a problem in the area of intimacy, it's 90 percent important."

All of us know that any two people can have sex, but not every "couple" knows true intimacy. The physical act, as important and enjoyable as it is, must not be the primary focus. Those who are in right relationship with God know there is a spiritual and emotional component to the act of marriage that must not be overlooked.

Men and women do look at the sexual relationship differently. Generally speaking, women desire a sense of connectedness. Men, while they may enjoy an emotional bonding, usually focus more fully on the physical sense of being co-naked.

1. Take a few moments and go back and review what husbands and wives said about sexual intimacy in their marriages (see pages 63-66). As you read these comments, stop and discuss any of them that express your own sentiments about the subject.

The Cornerstone of Sexual Fulfillment

2. Matthew 19:6. A couple will never know true intimacy unless there is true commitment. An exclusive husband/wife relationship that is ordained by God is the *only* way to satisfy the longing for oneness that is innate in every couple.

Commitment to Stay

3. Matthew 19:6 says, "What therefore God has joined together, let no man separate." Have the two of you, since your wedding day, recommitted your marriage to the Lord? Before you go any further, stop for a moment. Take each other's hands, look each other in the eye, and repeat these words to each other:

My gift from God,
I'm grateful for you
And for all this time we've been together.
And from my heart
I pray that the years ahead
Will be many.
In the time that has passed
I know there are joys
That have been overshadowed
By ways I have hurt you.
For this I ask you to forgive me.
And on this day
I recommit my love and devotion to you
And I ask the heavenly Father
To help me be His light to you
To our family
And to those around us.
With God as my help—I will.

Signed_____

Signed_____

    Date_____

Commitment to Purity

Being committed to stay is essential, but it's not enough. There must also be a firm commitment to stay pure within the marriage. Fidelity to one another is the promise to never go to or allow anyone else to fulfill the sexual needs of the other. That fidelity includes the elimination of pornography of any kind (Internet, magazine, movies, romance novels, soap operas). Anything that feeds your sexual needs outside of the marriage is unfaithfulness.

4. Read together Hebrews 13:4. The admonition to keep the marriage bed undefiled is often interpreted as "the marriage bed cannot be defiled." Consequently, couples mistakenly think anything they do, as long as it's in the marriage bed is fine. That's not what that passage says. It says, "Don't defile it." For instance, anything that physically hurts a mate is not right. Forcing a spouse to violate his or her sense of conscience is not loving. And, of course, bringing in a third party, either in the form of another person, a person on the screen, page, or in the imagination defiles the marriage bed.

Our commitment to keeping the marriage pure is one that results in a sense of safety, comfort, warmth, and oneness. That, my friends, is the recipe for tremendous physical enjoyment.

Commitment to Satisfy

5. Does God have anything to say about sexually meeting the needs of our spouse? Read 1 Corinthians 7:3-5; Proverbs 5:15-21; and the entire book of Song of Solomon.

When we learn to fully love and satisfy our spouse, we are joining in agreement with God. It was He who designed the physical parts of our bodies to join together in such a way as to illustrate the closeness and intimacy that can only be known in the purity of the marriage bed. Anything other than a loving, physical union that celebrates God's design and God's desire for husbands and wives to know unadulterated pleasure is just the sex act. And that's not special—any dog or cat can do it.

Chapter Six

I Need a Friend

What husbands and wives aren't telling each other about the hunger for a friend:

> *"Yes, I need for you to be my lover, but I also need a friend! I miss having fun with you."*

There's nothing more lonely than sharing a bed with someone, and yet not sharing his or her life. Many of the husbands and wives we questioned were greatly saddened by the lack of companionship they felt toward their mates.

1. Is your spouse someone whom you can "what if" with (see page 79)?

2. Do you miss having fun with your mate?

3. List some of the fun activities you and your beloved used to do before you got married.

   •

   •

   •

4. Assuming these activities were not sinful, what's keeping you from resuming some of them?

5. Go through the acrostic F-R-I-E-N-D-S-H-I-P with your spouse. Discuss each letter and how you can incorporate some of your own ideas into a fun pact.

6. Take a look at the "R" in friendship—respect one another with your words. Read these passages. How do your words affect your marriage?

   Proverbs 12:18—

   Proverbs 18:21—

   Proverbs 25:11-16—

7. Are there any changes that need to be made in how you speak to one another? Do you use the three-question rule before you say something to each other: Is it true? Is it kind? And is it necessary?

8. Complete this sentence and talk about it with each other.

"I love it when my wife says…"

"I love it when my husband says…"

Plan an evening out, just the two of you. Use the conversation starters given (on page 96), or create your own.

10. Write your own words of appreciation for your mate. It doesn't have to be long or elaborate. If you need some ideas, go to the store and spend a few minutes in the greeting card section. Read some of the lovely verses and adapt them to your thoughts and feelings. Give your personal card or letter to your beloved. That little bit of effort and sensitivity could spark some "fun" in your marriage.

Chapter Seven

Making a Living or Making a Killing

"We need to make a change in our fiscal focus. The pressure to achieve financial success and to accumulate and pay for all our possessions is hurting our marriage. I don't want to fight about money anymore. I want to make it our goal, as a couple, to be satisfied with making a living, instead of trying to make a killing."

Money is all right, but you have to waste a lot of time to make it." Some couples find themselves with more time than money, while others have money but no time for what is really important. Both situations are sad because each one has given money an enormous amount of power.

The husbands and wives we questioned had much to say about how money and the time it takes to make it affects their marriage and ultimately their family. Together, read over the comments listed (see pages 104-108). Mark the ones that remind you of your situation.

Remember money issues are never about the money. It's always a bigger and more difficult predicament than just a matter of crunching numbers.

1. Assess your particular struggle with money. Do you run out of cash at the end of the month? Or is excess of money your quandary?

2. Read these passages together. What does God have to say about money?

1 Timothy 6:6-17—

Malachi 3:8-11—

2 Corinthians 9:6-11—

3. What is the prevailing attitude in your financial situation? Are you and your spouse content to make a living, or are you in pursuit of making a killing?

4. How has this attitude affected your marriage?

5. Does laziness have anything to do with your financial difficulties?

6. What level of material success would you be content with? How much money is "enough"? On a scale of 1 to 10 how much does money determine your happiness?

7. How close are the two of you in attitude when it comes to material success? Discuss your differences and your similarities.

8. How does your indebtedness (if applicable) affect your marriage relationship? If it causes stress, what can you do to alleviate the problem?

9. Are the two of you willing to do what it takes to be free from the slavery of debt?

Chapter Eight

Lead or Get Out of the Way

What husbands and wives aren't telling each other about the assigned roles for spiritual leadership:

> Wives: *"It is very important to me that our family have effective spiritual leadership. If you will not do the job, then I suppose I will have to do it myself. That's not what I want, but the spiritual health of our home is dependent on it, and it is too crucial to leave undone."*

> Husbands: *"I know I should be the spiritual leader of our home, but I don't know how, and I don't feel equipped or worthy of the job. But if you want me to lead, then you must step aside and let me try."*

It has long been assumed that regular church attendance is good for the soul, but did you know it was beneficial to the actual heart? A study conducted by Dr. George W. Comstock, a medical researcher for Johns Hopkins University, Department of Epidemiology, discovered that men, in particular, who attended church services at least once a week or more, reduced their risk of fatal heart disease by almost half. Also, if an individual, man or woman, observed the clean lifestyle associated with church attendance, they significantly lowered the incidences of other major diseases such as arteriosclerotic heart disease, cirrhosis of the liver, tuberculosis, cancer of the cervix, chronic bronchitis, fatal one-car accidents, and suicides.[5]

Even without the additional scientific information offered by Dr. Comstock, it has long been accepted that individuals, couples, and families of all sizes do better when they are surrounded by people whom they love and who love them.

The spiritual health and spiritual leadership of the family is a subject that provoked strong, immediate responses from those couples we questioned. For the most part, the women longed for their husbands to take the God-given responsibility to lead and direct the family in spiritual matters. Many of the husbands, on the other hand, voiced a feeling of inadequacy and guilt over their lack of spiritual leadership skills.

The Higher Purpose

1. Read together the following passages that are a reminder of the higher purpose God has designed for the marital union. What things can you do that will help you love one another more fully and, thus, fulfill God's word?

Psalm 4:6-8—

Ephesians 5:22-28—

Colossians 3:18-19—

1 Peter 3:1-7—

2. Read Hebrews 4:12 and Psalm 119:98-104. Diagnose what place God's word has in your life as a couple.

3. Do you have a consistent time when the two of you share the scriptures together? If not, what would be the best time to begin? Would reading an "every-day devotional book" help get you started and keep you on track?

4. Looking back over your years, can you recount a time when God answered a specific prayer the two of you prayed together?

5. Discuss together any needs the two of you have as a couple or as a family. List five specific things you need to bring before the Lord.

•

•

•

•

•

6. Now pray, believing and trusting that God hears and answers your prayers (Matthew 7:7-12). Make your request known to God. Keep a journal of your prayer requests. Make a note of what the prayer was and the date you prayed. After God answers your prayer, write down the date He responded.

7. Make a nightly devotional time a routine with your children. Turn off the television, and sit down as a family. Read a short Bible passage or story, and then let the children pick a song for the family to sing. Pray a prayer of thanksgiving for the day and protection for the night.

8. Read Hebrews 10:23-25 and 2 Timothy 2:22 together. If you don't attend a good, Bible-believing, Christ-preaching church, begin this Sunday to find one. Don't let another week go by without making it a priority to find a church family.

Chapter Nine

A Regret-Free Marriage

All sin is regretful, but not all regrets are sinful.

What husbands and wives aren't telling each other about being free from the past:

> "I love you and want to show you how I feel. However, there's a part of me that can't reach out to you because I am holding on to merciless regrets. My emotional paralysis has nothing to do with what you have done. I am the one who must deal with the pain from my past. As you pray for me and support my pursuit of God, I am confident I will find peace."

Being free from the regrets of the past is essential to moving on and embracing life with our spouses. Like having our hands cuffed behind our backs, regrets and pain from the past can hold us as prisoners. Only when we are ready to face the remedies of regret can we truly reach out to those we love.

1. Take a look at the regrets the husbands and wives listed on pages 142-147. With your spouse, discuss which ones, if any, are pertinent to your lives.

2. Which regrets that hold your heart hostage could be considered "avoidable"?

3. Are there sins that have produced terrible consequences that you need to confess and forsake?

4. Read Psalm 51 together and discuss how King David dealt with his avoidable regrets.

   • Godly sorrow for his sin

   • Confession of sins committed

   • Turning away from sin

   • Asking for forgiveness

   • Restored back to God's good favor

   • Rejoicing in salvation

   • Willingness to teach others from the lessons learned

Chapter Ten

Vintage Wine or Vinegar?

What husbands and wives aren't telling each other about their expectations as love matures:

> *"After these many years of being married to you, I want you to know the best is yet to come. I want us to fully enjoy every minute we have left together. I want our relationship to deepen and grow sweeter. I am willing to do whatever it takes to enrich our lives together until we get to that "old love" era. And maybe, by being a couple whose marriage is sweet to the taste of our children and grandchildren, they, too, will want what we will have."*

There are two categories of widows—the bereaved and the relieved. As humorous as this little quip might be, it does reveal a profound choice. What kind of memory will we bequeath to those we leave behind?

Those of us who have children, and even grandchildren and great-grandchildren, have a keen responsibility to leave a legacy of love worth imitating. The challenge to us all is, Will the endowment of marriage we leave to those who follow after us be a recollection of devotion and affection that is sweet and satisfying (vintage wine)? Or will it be a remembrance of cutting, sharp remarks and bitter dispositions (vinegar)?

Passing the Sweet Cup

1. Read the following passages together and discuss how, as a couple, you can help your cup of love remain full and sweet.

   • Proverbs 16:21-24

   • Proverbs 15:4

   • Proverbs 24:1-4

   • Psalm 91:15,16

   • Psalm 51:17

2. Looking back on your early years of marriage, what seemed so important at the time but now doesn't seem like such a big deal?

3. What advice would you offer to young couples getting married today?

4. Discuss what you dread most about growing older.

5. What can the two of you do together to keep your marriage sweet and satisfying? List three things that you can do *this* week.

•

•

•

Notes

Chapter 1: Prepared, Repaired, Paired

1. Steve Chapman, "We," Times & Seasons Music, BMI, 2001. Used by permission.
2. Steve Chapman, "This House Still Stands," Time & Seasons Music, BMI, 2000. Used by permission.

Chapter 2: I Need a Teammate, Not a Cell Mate

1. Steve Chapman, "I Need You," Times & Seasons Music, BMI, 1993. Used by permission.
2 .Heidi Chapman Beall, "It's You," Times & Seasons Music, 2000. Used by permission.

Chapter 3: A Partner, Not a Parent

1. James Walker, *Men Who Won't Lead and Women Who Won't Follow* (Minneapolis: Bethany House Publishers, 1989), p. 21.

Chapter 4: The Challenge of Change

1. Steve Chapman, "Who Are You?" DawnTreader Music, 1984. Used by permission.
2. Steve Chapman, "The Drive from Austin," Times & Seasons Music, BMI, 1993. Used by permission.
3. Steve Chapman, "Much Too Quiet," Times & Seasons Music, BMI, 1998. Used by permission.
4. Nathan Chapman, "Nathan's Response," Times & Seasons Music, BMI, 1998. Used by permission.
5. Steve Chapman, "Making Room for Sarah," Times & Seasons Music, BMI, 1993. Used by permission.
6. Steve Chapman, "The Pages Turn," Times & Seasons Music, BMI, 1996. Used by permission.

Chapter 5: Connected or Co-Naked

1. Steve Chapman, "The Ships Are Burning," Times & Seasons Music, BMI, 1996. Used by permission.
2. Steve Chapman, "What I Wouldn't Give," Times & Seasons Music, BMI, 2001. Used by permission.
3. Steve Chapman, "Faithful to You," Times & Seasons Music, BMI, 1997. Used by permission.
4. Steve Chapman, "Metal," Times & Seasons Music, BMI, 2002. Used by permission.
5. Nathan Chapman, "You Take My Breath Away," Times & Seasons Music, BMI, 1999. Used by permission.

Chapter 6: I Need a Friend

1. Steve Chapman, "The Loneliest One," Times & Seasons Music, BMI, 2002. Used by permission.
2. Steve Chapman, "Bother My Baby," Times & Seasons Music, BMI, 1998. Used by permission.

3. Steve Chapman, "When Memories Turn to Gold," Times & Seasons Music, BMI, 1998. Used by permission.

4. Steve Chapman, "Love Song of the Hunter," Times & Seasons Music, BMI, 2001. Used by permission.

5. Dr. Victor Frankl, *Man's Search for Meaning* (New York: Pocket Books, 1969), pp. 68-69.

6. Probably adapted from "Love," by Roy Croft. The clipping on file doesn't include the author's name. The line "I love you not for closing your ears to the discords in me, but for adding to the music in me by worshipful listening" is not part of Croft's poem.

Chapter 7: Making a Living or Making a Killing

1. Steve Chapman, "Not the Ring," Times & Seasons Music, BMI, 2003. Used by permission.

2. John MacArthur, *New Testament Commentary: Matthew* (Chicago: Moody Press, 1985), p. 418.

3. Steve Chapman, "Where I Live," Times & Seasons Music, BMI, 1996. Used by permission.

4. Steve Chapman, "All I Should Owe," Times & Seasons Music, BMI, 1993. Used by permission.

5. Mickey Cates, "The Good Years," DawnTreader Music, SESAC, 1987. Used by permission.

Chapter 8: Lead or Get Out of the Way

1. Steve Chapman, "Wednesday's Prayer," Times & Seasons Music, BMI, 1998. Used by permission.

2. Steve Chapman, "Precious Moments," DawnTreader Music, SESAC, 1989. Used by permission.

Chapter 9: A Regret-Free Marriage

1. Steve Chapman, "There Is Good News," Times & Seasons Music, BMI, 1992. Used by permission.

2. Steve Chapman, "The Guide," Times & Seasons Music, BMI, 2002. Used by permission.

3. Steve Chapman, "No Regrets," Times & Seasons Music, BMI, 1990. Used by permission.

Chapter 10: Vintage Wine or Vinegar?

1. Steve Chapman, "Old Love," Times & Seasons Music, BMI, 2001. Used by permission.

2. Steve Chapman, "Let Me Take Her Home," Times & Seasons Music, BMI, 1997. Used by permission.

A Talkative Quiet Time for Couples

1. John MacArthur, *New Testament Commentary: 1 Corinthians* (Chicago: Moody Press, 1984), p. 338.

2. Ibid., p. 339.

3. Ibid., pp. 340-41.

4. Ibid., p. 342.

5. Paul Lee Tan, *Encyclopedia of 7700 Illustrations* (Rockville, MD: Assurance Publishers, 1979), p. 241.

Songs Available

Chapter 1

Song: "We"
Album: Miles—SACD 1020
S&A Family, Inc

Chapter 2

Song: "I Need You"
Album: This House Still Stands—SACD 131
S&A Family, Inc

Song: "It's You"
Album: Long Enough to Know—SACD 375
S&A Family, Inc

Chapter 4

Song: "Who Are You?"
Album: Kiss of Hearts—SACD 8000
S&A Family, Inc

Song: "The Drive from Austin"
Album: Waiting to Hear—SACD 30
S&A Family, Inc

Song: "Much Too Quiet"
Album: At the Potter's House—SACD 110
S&A Family, Inc

Song: "Nathan's Response"
Album: At the Potter's House—SACD 110
S&A Family, Inc

Song: "Making Room for Sarah"
Album: Waiting to Hear—SACD 30
S&A Family, Inc

Song: "The Pages Turn"
Album: Chapters—SACD 75
S&A Family, Inc

Chapter 5

Song: "The Ships Are Burning"
Album: Kiss of Hearts—SACD 8000
S&A Family, Inc

Song: "What I Wouldn't Give"
Album: Miles—SACD 1020
S&A Family, Inc

Song: "Faithful to You"
Album: Kiss of Hearts—SACD 8000
S&A Family, Inc

Song: "Metal"
Album: Miles—SACD 1020
S&A Family, Inc

Song: "You Take My Breath Away"
Album: Long Enough to Know—SACD 375
S&A Family, Inc

Chapter 6

Song: "The Loneliest One"
Album: (Not yet released)
S&A Family, Inc

Song: "Bother My Baby"
Album: Steppin' in the Tracks—SACD 1250
S&A Family, Inc

Song: "When Memories Turn to Gold"
Album: Family Favorites—SACD 105
S&A Family, Inc

Song: "Love Song of the Hunter"
Album: Long Enough to Know—SACD 375
S&A Family, Inc.

Chapter 7

Song: "Not the Ring"
Album: Miles—SACD 1020
S&A Family, Inc

Song: "Where I Live"
Album: Chapters—SACD 75
S&A Family, Inc

Song: "All I Should Owe"
Album: Waiting to Hear—SACD 30
S&A Family, Inc

Song: "The Good Years"
Not available

Chapter 8

Song: "Wednesday's Prayer"
Album: At the Potter's House—SACD 110
S&A Family, Inc

Song: "Precious Moments"
Not available

Chapter 9

Song: "There Is Good News"
Album: Family Favorites—SACD 105
S&A Family, Inc

Song: "The Guide"
Album: Steppin' in the Steps—SACD 1250
S&A Family, Inc

Song: "No Regrets"
Album: Family Favorites—SACD 105
S&A Family, Inc

Chapter 10

Song: "Old Love"
Album: Long Enough to Know—SACD 375
S&A Family, Inc

Song: "Let Me Take Her Home"
Album: The Family Heritage Collection—SACD 3 PK
S&A Family, Inc

To order these albums, get information on concerts,
or book a concert, write or call:

S&A Family, Inc.
PO Box 535
Madison, TN 37116
(615) 382-9106

or check out Steve and Annie's website:

www.steveandanniechapman.com

114564